Margaret
Queen of Scotland

Margaret
Queen of Scotland

Henry Grey Graham

LEONAUR

Margaret Queen of Scotland
by Henry Grey Graham

First published under the title
St Margaret Queen of Scotland

Leonaur is an imprint of Oakpast Ltd
Copyright in this form © 2011 Oakpast Ltd

ISBN: 978-0-85706-455-4 (hardcover)
ISBN: 978-0-85706-456-1 (softcover)

http://www.leonaur.com

Publisher's Notes

The opinions of the authors represent a view of events in which he
was a participant related from his own perspective,
as such the text is relevant as an historical document.

The views expressed in this book are not necessarily
those of the publisher.

Contents

To All the Scots
Who Have Inherited
or
Embraced the Faith
of St Margaret
Queen of Scotland

Preface

Scotland is not over-rich in saints, or, to speak more correctly, in saints enrolled in the Universal Calendar. And the reproach is sometimes made, half humorously, that its only canonised saint among women—she whom Pope Innocent IV. raised to that honour in 1250, and whose life here follows—came from England. Reasons could easily enough be given to account for the dearth, or, at least, the obscurity, of Scottish saints. Meantime, the fact itself makes St Margaret all the more precious to us. She shines as a bright particular star. There is no Scot, whatever his creed, but is proud that his country, in the days of its independence, numbered her among its queens.

The story of St Margaret of Scotland, and of what she, a most devoted child of the Catholic Church, achieved for God and her country, can never be told too often. One would fain hope that the biography here presented may fall into the hands of many who profess not the faith of St Margaret. It gives, indeed, a most admirable picture of the Saint in her heroic practice of virtue and piety, and this is the principal thing. It will enkindle and inflame devotion to her in every Catholic breast, and incite to imitation. It could not indeed be otherwise: her piety was so attractive. The present biographer has not failed to indicate in due season the points wherein she may and should be imitated. Prior Turgot, her confessor, and afterwards Archbishop of St Andrew's, tells us somewhere in the *Life* of his royal penitent, which has been relied upon throughout as a prime authority, that her profound contrition and her shedding of tears at the most trivial imperfection often compelled tears from his own eyes.

But this book does more than that. It shows St Margaret to us as a true reformer—and in this respect she resembles not distantly both St Theresa and St Catherine of Siena—accomplishing, virtually alone, much-needed improvements in the condition both of Church and

State, without disturbing the constitution of either. And withal she stands before us as a model queen and mother, ruling well her house and kingdom, and lifting Scotland to a height of prosperity till then unknown. Interspersed judiciously throughout the narrative and illustrating it, we meet with brief sketches of contemporary history, so that the attentive reader will not only learn to love Margaret, but will see the men and manners and events of the period living again before him on every page.

Moreover, it may not be amiss to add, that in our days such a book as this has a special value, as showing what great things one frail woman can accomplish, provided only she be at once submissive to the authority of Holy Church and at the same time strive earnestly after the perfection the Church requires of all her children.

Henry Grey Graham.

Mother Well, Espousals of Our Lady, 1911.

Introduction

Fife is the "Land of St Margaret." Its ancient town of Dunfermline was her favourite home for over twenty years; she was married in the old Tower; and several of her children were born there. It is long ago—eight centuries and more—since the good Queen's sweet face and kind heart made sunlight in its people's homes; but the atmosphere is full of her still. There are the ruins of the royal dwelling; there, all that remains of the beautiful Abbey Church, built by St Margaret and great-headed, great-hearted Malcolm, her husband; and there, too, is her tomb, empty these three hundred years. It is an immense double plinth of grey marble, no longer in its place of honour within the church but outside in the churchyard, in all that is left of the ancient Lady Chapel.

The great Presence is gone from the stately church and St Margaret's relics are gone, too. Her sacred bones no longer rest in Fife, either in the church or beneath that huge grey stone. When John Knox's rabble were abroad on their work of destruction the Catholics of Fife feared that their dear Saint's remains might suffer desecration, and so, with loving care, they removed them to a place of safety. The destroyers came, and expended their fury on the marble, as the marks of the hammers still show; but the sacred relics were beyond the power of their malice. And after three hundred years, the empty tomb with every other memorial of the holy Queen, is dear to the people of her own Dunfermline, in spite of the faithlessness of their fathers to the Church of St Margaret.

In the eleventh century, Fife was a rugged land of hills and glens. There were green slopes and great expanses of moorland covered with gorse and heather; as well as densely-wooded forest land extending, in some parts, down almost to the sea. It was an ideal hunting-ground:

tradition tells that Malcolm Canmore found it to be such; and also that it was on the occasion of a successful hunting expedition that he discovered the beautiful glen of Pittencrieff, and chose it for the site of a royal dwelling. Mercer, a local poet, tells how the Celtic king, charmed with the wild grandeur of the place, and noting with his practised eye its great natural strength, made his sudden but momentous decision:—

> *"Here to the brim a goblet fill!"*
> *He cried, and stood upright;*
> *"This to our fort upon the hill,*
> *Soon may it rise to sight,*
> *Unblotted ever be its fame,*
> *And aye Dunfermline be its name."*

When St Margaret came to Scotland the Tower of Dunfermline was Malcolm's favourite residence. It stood on the most precipitous part of a small peninsula formed by the windings of a rippling burn, and was almost aggressive in its strength. Built for safety rather than for beauty, it was surrounded by rocks and cliffs and forest land; and alone in its glory, for the church and palace were things of the future, it looked proudly down over uplands and valleys to the distant sea, that then as now shimmered like liquid silver in the sunlight, or lashed itself into snowy foam, when the winds were high.

The paths trodden by St Margaret on her errands of love and mercy, are covered today by the streets of the busy town; and the wild fastnesses where Nature's beauty brought her so close to Nature's God, have long ago given place to house and garden and cultivated field. One sacred fragment of the old-time woodland has indeed been saved, in spite of the present-day tendency (at time of first publication), to cover every available space, in and about a town, with buildings. This is the wooded dell or "den," as it is called locally, in which is still to be seen the cave oratory of the holy Queen. Here she was wont to repair, alone and in secret, to spend hours in sweet communion with her Lord, with no eyes to see, except those of the angels.

The oratory is a natural cavern in the rock. It measures some ten feet by eight and about seven feet in height, and probably is little changed since St Margaret knelt within. All else is very different. In the eleventh century the silent woods were around, and the only sounds of human life came from the Tower on the hill. Now the busy streets of Dunfermline are close to the old-world cave, and the pilgrim who would fain dream himself back in the eleventh century is recalled to the twentieth by the tinkling bells of electric cars.

It was a devoted son of the ancient town and evidently a lover of St Margaret who saved this treasure for Dunfermline and Scotland. But for his zeal it would probably have shared the fate of too many of the relics of Catholic times and we should only be able to read that it once had been.

St Margaret's Cave is not a thing of the past. It can still be seen, but he who would see it must seek for it. "*Seek*" then "*and you will find,*" and, ere you leave the holy place, kneel and say a prayer for the conversion of Scotland, there, where St Margaret prayed the same prayer so well, long, long ago.

The dell where the cave is situated and the cave itself, with its holy well, is a favourite theme with local poets. One of them, Thomas Morrison by name, says of it:—

> *Quaint legends to our hearts endear*
> *Our sainted Scottish Queen:*
> *Alone, unseen, oft strayed she here*
> *In thoughtful mood, serene;*
> *Thus oft from yonder ancient towers*
> *She sought from pomp to dwell,*
> *And pondered o'er life's fleeting hours*
> *Beside her cherished well.*

This well, one of the many bearing St Margaret's name, may still be seen by the visitor to her cave; and there are Dunfermline people even in these sceptical days who drink of its limpid water with loving faith and thank the good Queen for consequent relief from pain.

Nothing now remains of Malcolm's "strong Tower" except its foundations, and the palace, built by St Margaret or her children, is only a picturesque ruin. To those of the old faith, however, the very ground is holy, and the stones of the ancient buildings have wondrous things to say to those who know how to listen. Their whispers are magical and transport us backward through the intervening centuries till we live again, not only in the land, but in the days of St Margaret. When we look at the Abbey, alas! the spell is broken, for we are reminded no longer of zealous building up, but of wicked breaking down.

The first church of the Holy Trinity, built by St Margaret and her husband soon after their marriage, gave place wholly or in part to a more splendid edifice, erected by their youngest son, David I.; and

13

this was further beautified and improved by Alexander II. in the thirteenth century. The splendid Gothic choir and transepts of Alexander's Church retained their beauty for three hundred years, when they fell before the fury of the vandals of so-called Reformation days, just as Scotland's earliest churches had fallen before the wild onsets of the Danes.

The Abbey church has been restored in modern times, but the nineteenth century building has little of the exterior majesty and none of the interior beauty of its predecessors. In the shadow of the pillars, perhaps, it is possible to dream for a while of glory passed away—of a great high altar with ornaments of gold and gleaming lights, and of priests in gorgeous vestments, offering to the God of Heaven and Earth, the supreme act of worship—the Sacrifice of the Mass. We may shut our eyes and listen a while to the deep-toned chanting of the monks; then bow our heads at the mystic hush of the Elevation, when the priest in Christ's place, says "*This is My Body; this is My Blood*," and God comes down again to earth to visit His people. Alas! It is but a dream! There is no Mass, no real Presence, no altar now in Dunfermline Abbey church. It is a Protestant place of worship and contains a reading-desk and a plain table, as well as a pulpit which is pointed out to visitors as a thing of beauty, but there are no suggestions of St Margaret, and those of her faith are glad to exchange the atmosphere of the modern church for that of the Abbey ruins.

When we have breathed the air that the good Queen breathed and lingered in the haunts she loved, until it seems that we live again in her far-off age, it is a wonder if we do not find ourselves wandering along the path by which she first came to Dunfermline, eight hundred years ago. It probably coincides for the most part with the broad, well-made road which leads to Queensferry; but the aspect of the country today, (at time of first publication), with its wealth of cultivated fields and prosperous dwellings, is very different from that presented to the eyes of the Saxon Princess in 1069, in the days when sower and sowing time were alike unknown in the fair land of Fife.

Queensferry is on the shore of the Firth of Forth, "the sea which separates Lothian from Scotia," as an ancient writer calls it, and which Queen Margaret crossed and recrossed many times on her journeys between Dunfermline and Edinburgh. Almost midway between the "ancient toon" and Queensferry there is a great stone on the hillside with many peculiarities of its own. St Margaret's Stone, as it is called, is well known throughout the country and it has many visitors, archaeologists and geologists as well as historians and simple lovers of the good Queen. It is perched on the crest of one of the undulations by which the land rises from the Forth to Dunfermline, and tradition tells how the Saxon Princess and her friends, weary of climbing the hill, rested here and waited for the coming of the Scottish King. As the fair exile leaned her head against the stone—her stone for ever after, in memory of its brief service—of what was she thinking? Did she ponder God's designs in this strange adventure and wonder where and how her wanderings were to end; or did she, thus early, get one of those strange glimpses into the future with which she seems to have been gifted in later life? It was the dearest wish of both Princesses, that they might be allowed to consecrate themselves to God in the religious life; and it may be, that sweet thoughts of the peaceful seclusion of the cloister, came to St Margaret as she prepared herself to meet these wild Scots, of whose fierce doings she had doubtless heard in her English home.

Scientific men think that St Margaret's Stone is a fragment of a "dolmen" or "cromlech," one of the peculiar stones used by the Druids of old in their mysterious rites. The Druids were long gone when St Margaret came, but she was to meet and combat some of their superstitions still. They lingered long in some parts of Scotland, dimming the radiant beauty of the Catholic faith. St Ninian, and later, St Columba, with his splendid army of apostles, had done glorious work and reaped an abundant harvest; but the inroads of the Danes had made sad havoc since their time. Ruined monasteries and slaughtered monks marked the progress of the Northmen through the country, for their hate was fiercest and their fury deadliest where they found Christianity flourishing. Small wonder, then, that the people were left like sheep without shepherds; and that the light, which had gleamed so brightly for a space, was already slowly fading.

God was in His Heaven, nevertheless, and it was not His will that Scotland should relapse into paganism. *After the night, the day returns* and Princess Margaret, seated by the Druids' Stone was the herald of the dawn. The ferry across the Forth is still the Queen's Ferry and the villages on its banks are named respectively North and South Queensferry. Thirty years ago the Queen's Ferry was a necessity and many remember the broken journey from Edinburgh to Aberdeen, when North British passengers had to leave the train for the boat and the boat for the train in order to cross the Forth. The great Forth Bridge, one of the triumphs of modern engineering science, spans the estuary today, and the train carries its passengers over the water with none of the ancient delays and inconveniences. The beautiful land-locked bay formed here by the waters of the Forth, has for hundreds of years borne the name of St Margaret's Hope. The lonely, gloomy ruin on the promontory is Rosyth Castle where dwelt of old the Stuarts of Rosyth. It has many interesting historical associations but they do not reach as far back as St Margaret's time.

One of her descendants, indeed, another queen beautiful and devoted to her faith as her great ancestress—poor unhappy Mary Stuart—made the Castle her first resting-place before crossing the Forth, after her flight from Lochleven. To those outside the "Kingdom of Fife" and perhaps not much interested in the history of the Scottish Queens, Rosyth was an unknown name a few years ago. Things are very different now, for the busy world is coming to St Margaret's Hope. The Government is establishing a naval port and base at Rosyth, and soon men-of-war will ride in the bay and a garden city spring up around its margin.

Somewhere on the shores of St Margaret's Hope, probably near the ancient castle, there is a hallowed spot—that on which the Saint's foot rested for the first time on Scottish soil. It was a happy step—happy for Scotland and happy for Margaret; Margaret was to make Scotland a truly Christian country and Scotland was to make Margaret a saint.

CHAPTER 1

Margaret in Hungary

St Margaret was born in Hungary about the year 1045. Her father, Edward the Stranger, was the younger son of Edmund Ironside, who shared the dominion of England with Canute, the Dane. When Edmund was treacherously murdered by Count Edric in 1017, Canute assumed the guardianship of his two sons, until, as he said, they should be old enough to succeed their father. The boys were sent to Sweden, some say, in order that they might quietly be despatched to a better world, and trouble Danish rule in England no more.

If such was Canute's design, the Swedish king was more humane. He was kind to the fatherless children and soon found some pretext for sending them to Hungary, where he was confident they would be protected by the saintly King Stephen. Nor was his confidence misplaced: the English princes were welcomed at the Court of Hungary as became their rank, and educated as carefully as if they had been members of the king's own family. The elder prince died before reaching manhood, but Edward was strong and healthy and grew up into a virtuous, accomplished and handsome young man. The king regarded him with much favour and willingly gave his consent to his marriage with his own queen's sister, the Princess Agatha.

Of this marriage, St Margaret was the eldest child. Later another daughter, Christina, was born to Edward and then a son, known in English history as Edgar Atheling. Prince Edgar naturally was the hope of his parents and the centre of all their ambitions and plans for the future; and yet, it was not he, but his beautiful elder sister, the Princess Margaret, whom God had destined to make the family glorious. Margaret's life was to make a mark on history which will endure for all time, while Edgar's was to pass like a shadow; and Margaret's children, not Edgar's, were to sit on the thrones of both England and Scotland.

Unfortunately, we have few details of St Margaret's childhood and the formation of her character; though we can judge of the sweetness of the blossom by the fragrance and beauty of the opened flower. The ancestors of the Princess, Saxon and Bavarian, had been distinguished for sanctity as well as for courage and wisdom. The blood of Alfred flowed in her veins and her mother was close in kinship to St Henry of Bavaria, while kings and queens of both races had laid aside sceptre and crown for the lowly life of monastery and convent. Margaret came of a race of saints, no less than a race of kings, and she was richly endowed with the noble attributes characteristic of both.

"*You have not chosen Me, but I have chosen you*" says our Lord, and Margaret's simple faith and whole-hearted love of God, showed from her earliest years that she was especially His own; though even her nearest and dearest never dreamt of the great work that she had to do for Him.

Nay, little maidens! We are not forgetting that St Margaret had sinners as well as saints among her ancestry; nor are we suggesting that she inherited only saintly qualities, and had no difficulties in serving God so faithfully. Like every other daughter of Eve excepting Our Lady herself:

Our tainted nature's solitary boast,

Princess Margaret had to fight against the world, the flesh and the devil; and she was not confirmed in grace either, but subject to defeat and failure even as we are. True, she was a born queen, a leader and ruler by nature, with all the power and decision and acceptance of responsibility that marks the great mind, but characters such as hers have weaknesses as well as strong points. If St Margaret shows none of these weaknesses, but goes on from day to day and year to year, growing in every womanly and queenly virtue, neither unduly elated by prosperity nor depressed by adversity, it does not prove that she had no battles to fight; it rather shows that she had learnt early to fight so silently and to triumph so entirely that those around should be unaware of the warfare. We are all possible saints but only those attain to sanctity who correspond with God's graces, and this is what St Margaret did so faithfully and so well.

Sow an act, reap a habit;
Sow a habit, reap a character;
Sow a character, reap a destiny.

This is the process for saint and sinner alike.

The court of Hungary in the eleventh century was a model of what a Christian court should be and the young princess was fortunate in her environment. The Princess Agatha was a wise and good mother and took care that her children should be brought up in innocence and simplicity. There must have been many occasions, too, for the practice of humility and the exercise of self-forgetfulness and self-control. These are not things that can be learnt in a day; and the saint and queen we know and love in her riper years, would never have been such a perfect mistress of them, but for the early lessons of the little royal maiden in Hungary, long years before.

When we consider Prince Edward's position and circumstances, it is easy enough to realise how St Margaret learnt so soon that God's Kingdom is the only enduring one and that as with her dying lips she reminded her children *"worldly prosperity and glory are but momentary."* He was an exile banished from home and kindred and entirely dependent on the bounty of strangers—kind and tactful bounty, though it was. The very name given to him by the Hungarians—Edward the Stranger—shows that he was a man apart, somewhat in the background among the proud and wealthy nobles of the country. His life was shadowed by his early wrongs, and his spirit crushed by his powerlessness to help himself; so that he lacked the self-confidence of others, who, though not his equals in birth, had the sure inheritance which he had not.

Princess Margaret learnt to read and write and to do wonderful things with her needle, while she lived at the Hungarian court, and perhaps she learnt other things, too,—lessons lightly given by the thoughtless, but bitter and painful for the learner. A gifted child like Margaret, with her keen sensitive intelligence, could scarcely have attained the age of twelve years without noticing the peculiarities of the position of her family and suffering from them. No doubt she had childish battles to fight and childish puzzles to solve with results that left a lasting impression on her mind. Sorrows and trials expand large hearts, so she looked around on her little world with ever widening sympathies and forgot herself in trying to make others happier.

It is a pity that we know so little of St Margaret's early years for it would be interesting to trace in detail, in the child, the high principles which ruled and ennobled the life of the woman and queen.

CHAPTER 2

Margaret in England

Retribution has seldom followed so closely on crime as when, in the eleventh century, the Danes revenged the Massacre of St Brice's Day, by the conquest of England. Ethelred the Unready, had acted in accordance with his name until his foreign neighbours in the Danelagh had grown too powerful for his liking, and then, yielding to unworthy counsellors, he committed the folly and crime that disgraced his name and brought ruin on his family. Sweyn of Norway, wild with anger and grief, for his favourite sister, Gunhilda, was among the slain, came down like a whirlwind on England and only left it when it was crushed and beaten. Poor Sweyn, dying of his grief, gave the fruits of victory to Canute his son; and so for over twenty years England was ruled by Danish kings.

Hardicanute, the third of England's Danish rulers, died childless in 1042; and the Norwegians, engaged in warfare elsewhere, found themselves unprepared for such an emergency. The English, as they now called themselves, rejoiced at the golden opportunity of restoring the Saxon dynasty and gave the crown to Edward, son of Ethelred the Unready, afterwards known as Edward the Confessor. This Edward had been an exile, like his kinsman and namesake, while the Danes ruled in England. Brought up by strangers in Normandy, as the other Edward had been in Hungary, and, like him, deprived unjustly of the inheritance of an earthly kingdom, he had thought the more of striving to win the kingdom of heaven. Noted for the sanctity of his life as a prince, he became still more holy as a king, and his palace was like a monastery rather than a court, so regular was the life of its inmates.

Edward would not be alone in prosperity, any more than he had been in adversity, and so, when he found himself securely settled on the English throne, he sent ambassadors to Hungary, graciously inviting Edward the Stranger and his family to come and make their home in England. It was a great event for the family of St Margaret. England was home, in spite of the fact that only Prince Edward himself had ever been there and that even he had scarce a recollection of his native land. They would be strangers no longer—dependent on strangers no longer, for Edward was the acknowledged heir to the English throne. Henceforward, he would be Edward the Atheling, next in importance in England to Edward the Confessor himself; and when that king should lay down the sceptre he would be King of England.

The Princess Agatha was a queenly woman with a queenly estimate of royal dignities and privileges; and no doubt she rejoiced at the turn events had taken and looked forward to a happy and splendid life. And so, with the good wishes of their many friends in Hungary and laden with valuable gifts from the King and Queen, Prince Edward and his family came to England. Princess Margaret was about twelve years old at this time—a beautiful child with a powerful intellect, pious and thoughtful and serious beyond her years; though with a wellspring of quiet happiness in her heart that made her a delight to all with whom she came in contact.

In those days children could scarcely be childish. They were strictly kept in the background, and had to be respectful and decorous in the presence of their elders. Self-control, perfect submission and prompt obedience were required of them whether they were princesses or maidens of low degree; and they were not allowed to express their opinions and decide things for themselves as freely as many little people do nowadays. This repression was sometimes severe; and natural vivacity and spontaneity suffered perhaps in some cases. It was not so with Princess Margaret, for she had a prudent mother and prudent mothers know what is best for their own little girls, no matter what the customs of the age may be.

Life at the English Court was probably much the same to St Margaret as life in Hungary had been, with the difference that she was a person of much greater importance, being close in kinship to the king. In both courts the Princess had examples of high virtue going hand in hand with high birth. Possibly Edward's was the more austere, but custom would have made the life of the royal maidens secluded in any case. Other young girls of noble birth were brought up with the princesses, and shared their studies and pastimes. They lived by rule under the somewhat strict supervision of the "Mistress of the Maidens," and were taught to conduct themselves with a dignity befitting their high station.

The day began with the household Mass, and there were other devotions in common in the course of the day. There were hours of study, too, and plenty of needlework and embroidery, with recreation at allotted times. It was a simple life but full of happiness and innocent mirth. The maidens had little society; for the court of Edward with its piety and unworldly atmosphere was not a gay one; and, of course, they had few books, for printing was then an unknown art, and every copy of a book had to be laboriously transcribed by hand.

There were plenty of manuscripts for study, however, and copies of the sacred writings in sufficient number; and many of the maidens attained to considerable skill in music. Minstrels were sometimes admitted to the ladies' bower, to entertain them while they worked, with lays of love or chivalry.

For still the burden of his minstrelsy
Was knighthood's dauntless deed
And beauty's matchless eye.

The days were busy ones, for idleness was accounted a snare of the enemy, and so each hour had its appointed occupation—prayer, work, play or sleep.

Princess Margaret had brilliant intellectual powers, and ample opportunities were given her for developing them, so that while yet a mere girl she was remarkable for her learning. The chaplains of Edward the Confessor were highly cultured and pious men and Margaret found among them able tutors as well as spiritual directors. She studied Latin and French and was also instructed in scripture and religious knowledge. Her judgment was sound and accurate and her mind had a deep spiritual bent, which made sacred studies peculiarly fascinating to her. She could reason, too, and though her logic often bespoke her sex, and made her usually grave preceptors smile, her conclusions were always right. She had the knack of reaching the goal at once by a direct route of her own, while others were laboriously following the windings of the ordinary road and sometimes losing their way by taking a wrong turning. There was no danger of wrong turnings for Princess Margaret, with her simple, humble faith, and so she went on storing her mind with the treasures of sacred lore, and unconsciously preparing herself for her future mission.

Young as she was, she had long ago given the great deep love of her heart to God alone and His will was the rule of her life in little things as in great. Worldly glory had no charms for her. She had seen for herself how uncertain and unstable it can be and had learnt to value it accordingly. She would dream of perfect love and bliss as the songs of the minstrels taught her to do, but she would look for it beyond this world where death, and disappointment, and the fickle wills of men, work such havoc with happiness.

Edward the Stranger was not the first prince to whom Edward the Confessor had shown hospitality. When Malcolm, the son of Duncan, King of Scotland, was driven from his own land by the murder of his father and the usurpation of Macbeth, he sought and found refuge and help at the English court. It was this very year when St Margaret's family came from Hungary, that Malcolm set out for Scotland with English troops behind him to win back his own. The English king had given him generous assistance and he made good use of it; Macbeth was killed at Dunsinane and Malcolm Canmore was crowned King of Scotland at Scone.

One chronicler tells that it was at this time that Princess Margaret was betrothed to Malcolm and that the promise of her hand was given by Edward the Confessor himself, but this seems very improbable from the age of the princess and still more so from the fact that Canmore, returning to his own land, married Ingibiorg of Sweden, widow of Earl Thorfinn. He was a widower, with a stalwart son when, fourteen years later, the Saxon royal family sought his hospitality, and possibly this was the occasion of his first seeing the Princess Margaret.

Poor Princess Agatha! If she was ambitious, as is hinted by historians, her high hopes were short-lived. Prince Edward, her husband, after only three days in his native land, fell ill and died and when she laid him to rest in St Paul's Church she buried with him her dreams of future greatness. True, she had a son; as far as hereditary rights were concerned, Prince Edgar was now the heir to the English throne; but then, neither the King nor the Saxon nobles looked favourably on the boy. He was a delicate youth—weak in intellect and character as well as in body and all unfitted by nature to be the ruler of a country like the England of those days—not long emerged from barbarism and composed of men of many races, still in the process of being welded into one nation.

Princess Agatha took her place at court indeed, and her son assumed the title of Atheling, but Edward the Confessor looked across the Channel to the friends of his boyhood and dreamed of a Norman successor; while the strong men of England rallied round the Saxon

Harold Godwin, as the worthiest and most capable among themselves. He was not of royal blood? No! But hereditary claims were not of such vital importance as they are now; and history affords many instances of the young and weak being set aside in spite of descent, in order that older or stronger men might govern.

The years flew past, but with their flight Prince Edgar's chances of succession grew more and more feeble while his mother's anxieties on his behalf became accordingly more keen. The situation in England was watched with interest by Harold Hardrada of Norway, who considered England his own, by right of inheritance from Hardicanute, and as Edward's life drew near its close, England was filled with rumours of warlike intentions on the part of both Norway and Normandy. A strong man in every sense of the word was needed as a successor to King Edward and poor Edgar Atheling was not strong in any sense.

Princess Margaret was growing into womanhood as her kinsman, the Confessor, worn out by austerities and the worry of State quarrels, which his peaceful soul abhorred, slowly sank into the grave.

It was her duty and privilege to share her mother's anxieties and to lighten them by her counsel and sympathy and so her mind and heart were all the time being trained for the sphere of greater guiding power and wider sympathies which was to be hers. Tall and stately and with the bearing of a queen, Princess Margaret was beautiful in face and form. She had the wonderful fairness that made St Gregory the Great say of the children of her country, that they were "*Angels not Angles*"; and her blue eyes reflected the selflessness and sweet serenity of her innocent soul. Princess Christina and she, had both leanings towards a life in the cloister; but, in the meantime, they waited until God's will in the matter should become more clear. The time was at hand when it was to be manifested for Princess Margaret at least, in no uncertain manner.

CHAPTER 3

Margaret in Scotland

Edward the Confessor died in 1066 and only a very few—the most enthusiastic lovers of the Saxon dynasty—thought of Edgar Atheling as his successor.

Harold Godwin was declared king by the Witan, and Prince Edgar's claims were set aside indefinitely; for the atmosphere was thick with rumours of war. Harold Hardrada, King of Norway, had landed in the north with an army, to claim the crown as the heir of Hardicanute; and Tostig Godwin, jealous of his brother's elevation to the throne had joined the enemy with a body of English malcontents. Meanwhile, reports came, fast following each other, of warlike activity in Normandy, where Duke William was raising a great army to invade England on the south.

The Duke urged as his claim that Edward the Confessor had promised him the crown, ignoring the somewhat important detail that the same crown, or the kingdom which it represented, was not a personal possession to be bequeathed by one man to another. The crown was at the disposal of the people, not of the dying king, but Duke William preferred to think otherwise and loudly declared that he was going to England to take what was already his own. Harold Godwin, according to the Duke of Normandy, was no king but a perjurer and a traitor, who had sworn solemnly on the relics of the saints to uphold the Norman claims to England and had broken his oath.

Whether Edward the Confessor made the promise attributed to him is uncertain; but we know very well that he loved French people and French ways and after Edward the Atheling's death, had inclined to Norman William as his successor. But Harold Godwin! English Harold! with no French sympathies whatever! Is it possible that he could have sworn to help the stranger to sit on the throne of England?

25

Improbable as it sounds Harold had so sworn but the oath was an unwilling one and taken under rather remarkable circumstances.

It happened in the Confessor's lifetime. Harold was cruising in the English Channel and during a sudden storm his vessel was driven on the rocks and wrecked off the coast of Normandy. Now, according to feudal usage, a wreck became the property of the lord of the domain on whose shores the vessel was stranded, and though there were saving clauses to safeguard the rights of the owners when there were survivors, such clauses were often disregarded. Harold was promptly conducted to the castle of one of the vassals of William of Normandy, where he was virtually a prisoner; and the wily Duke determined to use the mishap of this powerful English noble for his own advantage. Harold was treated with every courtesy until at length he spoke of returning to England and then he got an unpleasant surprise. Duke William showed him the opening of a terrible dungeon below the level of the sea and gave him a choice. He must swear on the relics of the saints to help the Norman to make himself king of England at the Confessor's death or be consigned to this living grave for the rest of his life. There was no help, for none in England would ever know but that he had perished by shipwreck. Poor Harold! there would have been no glory even in death.

Harold refused the dungeon, took the oath, and returned to England, but, once safe at home, he decided easily enough that an oath forced from him under a threat so terrible was not binding and when the Witan offered him the crown he accepted it without scruple. William did not fail to remind him of his oath but Harold answered only by defiance.

And now this king of a month had to defend his country against two sets of enemies at once. It seems a strange thing to us, but the Normans were scarcely taken seriously. It would be easy to deal with the French, said public opinion, if once the northern foes were vanquished.

To the north then went Harold with his brave Englishmen behind him and at Stamford Bridge the Norwegians were utterly routed. Tostig Godwin thus brought to his knees, humbly asked his brother's forgiveness for his unnatural conduct and it is to Harold's credit that this—one of his last acts—was merciful and generous; he readily forgave the rebel and loaded him with favours.

Exultant over their victory, the English nobles marched southward with high hopes. They would crush the ambitious Norman at a blow and all England would shout with joy over a double triumph. Harold alone had presentiments of evil. He knew better than any the strength and determination of the Norman and so he realised to a fuller extent, the magnitude of the task that lay before him.

The battle was fought at Hastings and all the world knows its issue. Harold was defeated and slain and Norman William became William the Conqueror and King of England. So complete was the conquest that when William was crowned in Westminster Abbey, within the year and with the consent of the Witan, most of the surviving English nobles attended the ceremony and among them was Edgar Atheling.

Probably the Princess Agatha hoped for a time that her family might still make a permanent home in England. There were brave men who were making a bold stand for her son as the representative of the ancient race of kings, and the Normans were not yet sure of their ground; besides, surely, at the worst, the Conqueror would be gracious and generous to the Saxon royal family who had lost all that he had gained. Whatever hopes the Princess had were vain. News came that the Conqueror was already arranging about the disposal of her property and the marriage of her daughters with Norman nobles; and she saw no way of escape from tyranny and injustice except night.

The ancient tradition represents the Princess as deciding to return to Hungary with her children, but modern writers say that her destination was Scotland and the court of Malcolm Canmore. Some go so far as to assert that she came by invitation, Malcolm having met Edgar Atheling in the North of England during the war of the previous months. It was evident in any case that Prince Edgar had given up, for the present at least, all hopes of ousting the Conqueror and whatever ending the Princess Agatha designed for her travels she left England with her three children in the autumn of 1069.

In time, for even a coasting voyage was a slow and tedious business eight centuries ago, the English vessel reached the shores of Scotland and then came a violent storm.

Those who have dwelt on the banks of the Forth can well imagine the plight of the strangers:—

The black'ning waves are edged with white,
To inch and rock the sea-mews fly;
The fishers have heard the water-sprite,
Whose screams forbode that wreck is nigh.

Thus Sir Walter Scott describes the coming storm on these very

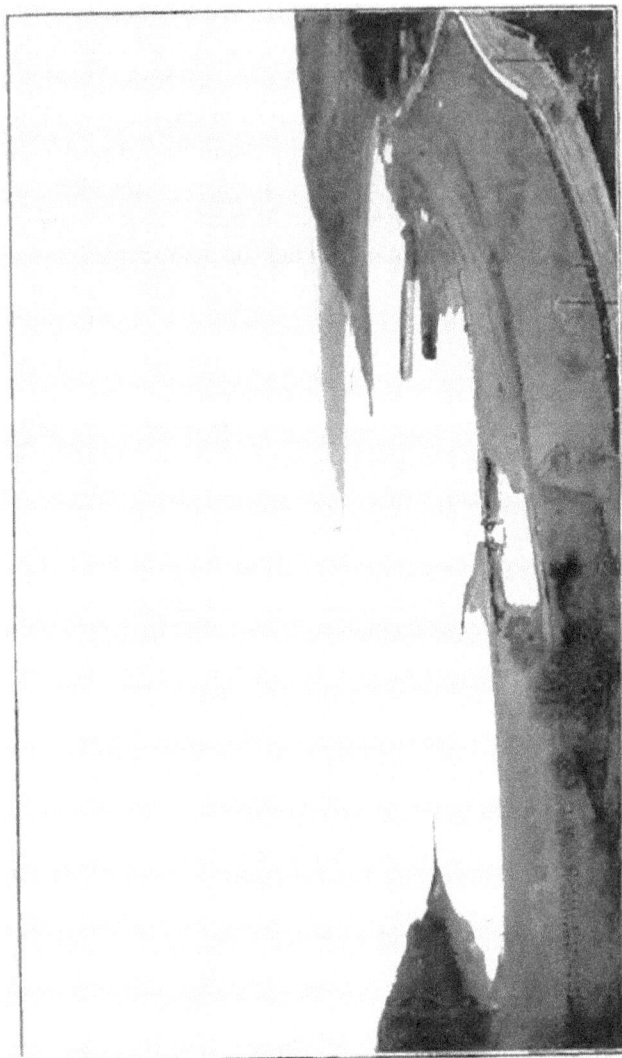

St Margaret's Hope

waters and though ordinary folks must disclaim the water-sprite, they cannot but own that the sights and sounds are weird enough to suggest it. Dark clouds leap out of nowhere and spread rapidly over the sky while a grey mist creeps eerily up from the sea to meet them. The distant hills, the green stretches of shore, the headlands, even the islands are gradually enveloped in its clammy folds and poor voyagers feel themselves *"alone on a wide, wide sea."* Then come wild gusts of wind and dashing rains and the vessel is driven this way and that till destruction seems inevitable.

How the English ship came into the Firth—whether by accident or design—matters little, It encountered the storm there, and, as the last gusts were dying away, took shelter, considerably the worse for its fight with winds and waves, in the bay that is now called St Margaret's Hope. The exiles, no doubt glad enough to leave the stormy waters, landed as soon as possible on the shores of the bay, probably in the vicinity of the promontory on which now stands the dreary ruin of Rosyth Castle.

To Malcolm Canmore in Dunfermline Tower, came the news of the English ship battling with the waves and later of the distinguished strangers landing on his soil and craving his hospitality. The chroniclers assure us that the messengers gave the Princess Margaret special mention, telling the King that she was tall and fair and praising "her incomparable beauty and the pleasantness of her jocund speech." It may be indeed that, writing in the light of after events, they were unconsciously biased by devotion to her who had by that time become their own Queen and Saint, for Princess Margaret was of minor importance among the little group of exiles. Her mother, the Princess Agatha, naturally took the lead and her brother Prince Edgar was considered the rightful King of England and esteemed accordingly.

And yet, it was Margaret whose name and story were to make Fife interesting to all succeeding generations, while her seemingly more important relatives were to live in Scottish history only for her sake and in as far as they were connected with her. If it was a seeming accident that sent the English ship to Rosyth, it was certainly God's design—one of those apparent chances fraught with mighty consequences, which are in reality simple effects of His Providence.

Malcolm's "wisest counsellors" says the chronicle, were at once despatched to the shores of the Forth to greet the strangers, bidding them welcome to Scotland in the King's name and inviting them to Dunfermline. The King, himself, the visitors were assured, was already on his way to meet them, that he might in person conduct them to his home.

Had Malcolm any misgivings as he made his preparations? He had lived at the court of Edward the Confessor and so he knew the differences between it and his own primitive palace. Nature indeed had done its best for his dwelling for he had had regard to beauty as well as strength of position in choosing its site. "That place," says Fordun, "was naturally well defended, being surrounded by a very thick wood and fenced by precipitous rocks in the middle of which was a pleasant level ground also strengthened by rock and water."

Beauty of position is not everything, however, and the Tower was a humble, lowly dwelling and all unlike a royal palace. Did Malcolm wish as he looked at its bare unsightly walls that he had thought somewhat more of state and elegance?

Canmore was the first king of a consolidated Scotland and the country was semi-barbarian still. The King and his rough nobles lived like their wild ancestors, almost entirely in the open air, war and the chase being at once their business and pastime. Houses were useful to them as affording shelter but they were certainly not ornamental, either without or within. Malcolm was a soldier well used to hardships and discomfort and so when he came back from the elegance of royal life in England, he did not seek to imitate it in his own land. He could fight battles better than furnish rooms, and though he knew how to appreciate order and beauty of arrangement, he was powerless to produce it. He was able to live without it too. He could maintain his power and extend it, by strength of intellect and the might of his brawny arm and so far he had been content enough with what life had given him.

He was not so narrow-minded as to pretend to despise the graces of civilisation because they were wanting in his own land, however; ignorance was his chief fault and that is a trifle when people are ready and willing to learn. Malcolm was both, and lo! as he strode down the hill from Dunfermline Tower a fair teacher awaited him by the Druids' Stone at Pitreavie.

It was in October that Princess Margaret came to Dunfermline. Probably when the storm had subsided and the winds were still, her first glimpse of Scotland was an agreeable surprise, for the woods are loveliest in autumn with all their wonderful variety of colouring; every shade of green and brown and red and gold intermingling in richest harmony. The Saxon Princess loved beauty of every kind, and perhaps the scenery as much as her own fatigue was the reason for the midway rest which has made the big stone famous for all time. The silver streak of the Forth lay at her feet, far down the green hill, with the islet of Inchgarvie, unburdened then with the support of the giant bridge of modern times; and across the sparkling waters in the distance could be seen the great rock of Edinburgh rising from radiant woods and crowned by the Maidens' Castle while more green hills met the sky as a background. It was fitting that Princess Margaret should look well at this land in all its wild beauty, for she had come, though she knew it not, to set in motion forces that would work a mighty change in the ages to come.

Autumn beauty is short-lived and winter is bleak and bitter in Scotland, even in our days of warm well-built houses, with heating and lighting apparatus almost perfect. There was little comfort in Malcolm's Tower at any season; but winter must have been dreary in the extreme, and Princess Margaret with her southern ideas cannot have found her first months in the north very enjoyable. There was no elegant tapestry in the Tower to cover unsightly walls, no delicate curtains and hangings of costly silk in hall or bower or bedchamber and no dainty vessels of silver and gold on the dinner-table. Many of the simple workers in Dunfermline's mills today, (at time of first publication), have more comfortable bedrooms and better laid tables than the Saxon Princess found in the dwelling of this eleventh century Scottish king.

It is one of the most remarkable evidences of Margaret's perfect selflessness, that she showed no sign of being ill at ease among her rude surroundings. Malcolm had all the sensitive pride of his race and if the beautiful princess had appeared unhappy or out of her element in his rough home, he would never have asked her to make it her own. That was not Margaret's way, however. She was no helpless maiden to languish because of untoward circumstances, or waste her time in self-pity. Difficulties showed her at her best because she always stood up to meet and master them. Perhaps she gloried, as saints often do, in her privations; more probably she never thought of self at all. There were others to be cared for and made happy, and Margaret had learnt from her infancy to think of self last.

She came like an angel of light into Malcolm's dull home and everything she touched was made beautiful. Her tact and womanly helpfulness smoothed away difficulties and brought order out of chaos; and while she gradually brought the whole household under her gentle sway, her winning ways and "jocund speech" made everybody love her and seek to do her will.

The master of the Tower was not an exception. There was no winter that year for Malcolm Canmore; the sun was shining all the time in his heart and home.

We know few of the circumstances of the engagement between the Celtic king and the Saxon princess, romantic as they seem to have been. The first thought of it comes with something like a shock, so unsuitable does it appear. It is easy enough indeed to understand Malcolm's love for Margaret. She was a royal maiden—royal in goodness and beauty as well as birth. He had seen her in difficult and untried positions and always to her advantage; ever self-possessed, serene and joyous, nothing disturbed the sweet peace of her soul.

For months she had been the angel of his household helping and cheering everybody, high and low, and the Tower would ever more be impossible as a residence without her bright presence.

It is not so easy to read what was taking place in Margaret's heart. Malcolm was old enough to be her father, and he was a widower, too, with a son who was no longer a child. He was a wild Celt only a little more civilised than his chieftains, with his interests centred in warfare and hunting; and little used to suit his language and manners to the company of gentle ladies. More- over, he was given to wild, fierce outbursts of anger, terrible to behold. While they lasted Malcolm was little better than his savage ancestors of a few centuries earlier, but happily they were of brief duration.

And yet we must give Canmore his due. He does not always get it in history, for the English only knew him in his savage moods, when he descended on them in one of his wild forays, burning and slaying like a very Dane. The Scots knew another and a different Canmore—a king who was wise in council as well as brave in battle and as true to his friends as he was fierce to his enemies—and Princess Margaret learnt to know him too. He had travelled further than most princes of his time and he was not uneducated though the chroniclers tell that he never learnt to read or write; for he could converse in Latin as well as in Saxon and Gaelic.

Appearance goes for something, too, and Malcolm was every inch a king. His huge body was formed in proportion to his great head, which, crowned with its ruddy locks, towered high above the giant warriors of his clans, and, terrible as his face appeared to Saxons south of the Border, it was full of kindliness and reverent admiration when it looked on Margaret. Perhaps with her acute perception, she saw more in Malcolm than others did, even in those first days—glimpses of natural refinement which only needed cultivation, possibilities latent within the simple giant's soul, such as he himself, not to speak of his neighbours, had never dreamed of.

The Princess had time during the long winter in the Tower to appreciate the sterling worth of the Scottish King and evidently she did so, for she was not an unwilling or reluctant bride. Once satisfied that this marriage was the will of God, she gave Malcolm a deep, abiding affection, which appears in all their after life, and which was the stronger and more beautiful because the love of God came ever first. There was a sigh all the same for the convent life which she had loved to picture as her own and which now must be relinquished. To the delight of the Scottish Court and with the approbation of Princess Agatha and Edgar Atheling, Malcolm Canmore, King of Scotland, and Princess Margaret of Hungary and England were united in marriage during the Eastertide of 1070.

"The nuptials were magnificently celebrated" says Fordun "at a place which is called Dunfermline, which the reigning king then held as a fortress."

Fothad, Bishop of St Andrew's, "ane man of great piety and learning" had the honour of uniting the distinguished couple, and Scotland's noblest sons and daughters were gathered together at Dunfermline for the marriage festivities. These occupied many days and were as splendid as Malcolm's love and generosity could make them. The minstrels sang of the beauty and goodness of the bride and of the valour and mighty deeds of the bridegroom, and there was no jarring note in the general harmony.

Even Nature seemed to share in the rejoicing, for Margaret's marriage was celebrated at an ideal time of the year—the month of April when winter's dullness and decay have given place to the awakening life of glad springtime. In the woods around the Tower, the trees were decking themselves in new robes of pale green, while golden primrose stars and blue violets peeped timidly out from their clustering leaves on the mossy ground. Overhead the birds sang joyously as they revelled in the delights of nest-building, and the world seemed a glorious place to live in. "*A bright beginning to a bright life*" sang the minstrels, and it would be well if marriage prophecies were always as true. There had been winter in Scotland since the coming of the Danes, but it was fast departing, and the sunshine of faith would fill the land again. Well may painters and poets vie with each other, making that wedding in the Tower famous alike on picture and in verse; for no other wedding before or since, in castle or in cottage, has brought so many blessings to Scotland.

CHAPTER 4

Margaret, Wife of Malcolm Canmore

Like a wise woman, St Margaret began her married life by putting her own house in order. She had not lived in Scotland for six months without seeing much that was amiss—abuses on every side crying aloud for remedy and reform. But then we must remember, St Margaret did not come as a reformer—as a female Alexander seeking worlds to conquer. She could not see the years to come with their manifold labours, and in her humility she did not dream of the great work that God had appointed her to do.

Do the duty that lies nearest thee,
The next will then have become clearer.

St Margaret was just a good woman living ever in God's presence and bent on doing well the duty of the moment. God unfolded His design before her eyes by degrees, and she was always ready for a movement onward and upward according to His will. That was all her scheme of reform, and probably it was also the explanation of her wonderful success. A proud "Sassenach" come North on purpose to improve and civilise would have met with dour opposition, barring her progress like the granite rocks of the Grampians, but St Margaret disarmed opposition by her humility and gentleness. She tamed her lions by love, and then led them after her like lambs. Malcolm was her first conquest, and none could have been more complete. His love and reverence for his beautiful wife grew with the years, and his whole nature was softened and sweetened by her influence, while impulses for good, hitherto dormant, began to make themselves felt, stimulated by her bright example.

It was not that Queen Margaret sought to rule her husband, or usurp his place; he was her lord and master, head of the kingdom and household alike, and she honoured him accordingly. Her power was *for rule, not for battle*, her genius for *sweet ordering, arrangement and decision*, and perhaps because of this true wifely attitude, she led her giant whither she would. Sir Noel Paton, one of Dunfermline's distinguished sons, has given us a beautiful picture of St Margaret. The young Queen is seated by her husband's side on a mossy bank, explaining the Scriptures from the book on her knee, while he listens in rapt attention. The painting is a labour of love, and not the first of the artist's tributes to St Margaret. Most of his early efforts had the good Queen as their subject, and Dunfermline values them now for her sake as well as for his.

Malcolm was indeed his young wife's pupil, and probably they often sat together as in the picture, for Scripture was always St Margaret's favourite study, but all the same that was not her ordinary method of instruction. She was too humble and too prudent to harass her fiery spouse with lectures on his life and duty, but she chose instead to live the Christ-life before his eyes day after day, proving in her own sweet self that holiness is the truest happiness. Malcolm saw and admired, and gradually began to imitate. He had hitherto thought that such virtue was only possible in monasteries and convents.

St Margaret's best chronicler, who is also her confessor, marvels at her wonderful union with God, and, good priest and monk as he was, felt himself unworthy to be her "soul's friend."

Some servants of God, when first strongly attracted to His service, have fear and awe in greater evidence, but "working out their salvation in fear and trembling," and so living ever in the great "Taskmaster's eye," they learn to love Him with all their hearts until *perfect love casteth out fear*. It was not thus with St Margaret. She could look back to no time of conversion, for she had given God her heart from her very childhood, and had never taken back the gift. Because she loved Him, she spent herself gladly in His service, and found His yoke sweet and His burden light. Our Lord's beautiful life on earth was her model, His own words, "*Be ye perfect as my Heavenly Father is perfect*," her standard of sanctity, and so it was a joy to her to live a life of prayer and penance and work.

Perhaps for this reason her austerity had nothing rigid or forbidding about it. She lived her heroic life with such freedom and simplicity, and found so much pure happiness in it, that others were attracted in spite of themselves and drawn to taste the sweetness of seeking first the Kingdom of Heaven.

Queen Margaret was a perfect wife, and Malcolm appreciated her value. Except in questions of war, when the fierce blood of the Gael surged up in him with a force too powerful, even for her influence, her slightest wish was his law. She had a genius for getting her own way with him and others, but she was sweetly masterful and never dogmatic or domineering. Stately and dignified always, there was nothing haughty or imperious about the good Queen. Her strength of will had no self-will in it, and none could submit and give up her own opinion more gracefully than she. Thus it was that people yielded to her, they knew not why, and in all her changes and improvements she made no enemies and evoked little criticism except wondering comments on her unfailing energy and undaunted courage.

The ancient chroniclers love to dwell on the relations between the rugged Scottish king and his winsome Saxon wife. They speak of her sunny face, her witty speech, her "infinite variety," and notice Malcolm's half-wondering delight in her presence and her doings. He is constantly finding something new to admire and love in this bright spirit, who has come into his life as from another world, filling it with joys hitherto unknown and unthought of. He loves her books just because she loves them, though, strange to say, he never learns to read them. He is often seen to take them tenderly in his hands, reverently kissing the page that his wife has been reading.

Sometimes the Queen misses a book for several days and then finds it in its place again, magnificently bound and ornamented with gold and precious stones. Book-binding had been an art among the Scots when they first came to Dalriada, and succeeding generations had brought it to great perfection, so there was at least one thing, at once Celtic and beautiful, that Malcolm could offer his Saxon Queen. Not once but many times did St Margaret thus discover a favourite volume arrayed in gorgeous new attire, and Canmore took care to be present at the finding, that he might enjoy his wife's delight in her treasure, now doubly valuable.

After years of married life the royal pair were still on the same playfully affectionate terms with each other, and ancient writers quaintly marvel that domestic happiness should continue so long unclouded. There came exceptionally severe winters when cold and famine made sad havoc among the poor, who were all too numerous in those primitive times; and the Queen could not be happy while they were suffering. She would sell her own beautiful garments and jewels that she might have wherewith to feed and clothe all who sought her help; and when her resources failed Malcolm was required to come to her aid. It was his joy to supply her wants, and prudence had to stand aside and be silent more than once while the royal treasury was well-nigh drained. The Queen introduced variety even into her appeals for the poor, for in periods of distress these appeals were so frequent that they might easily have become wearisome and monotonous.

Sometimes she would pretend to steal what she wanted, and nothing pleased her simple Gael better than to catch her in the act. He would take her small hand, money and all, in his own great horny one and lead her to her confessor, asking him how a little thief caught red- handed like this ought to be punished. He was in the habit of laying aside several gold pieces for the offertory at Sunday Mass, and St Margaret often confiscated some of these for her poor. When the King discovered his loss he invariably pretended to be hugely scandalised, and with great enjoyment of the situation would playfully threaten the Queen with trial and conviction. He never required restitution, however, and sometimes he would demonstrate the superiority of his own gigantic hand for thieving purposes—a superiority which his wife was ready to admit and use to the advantage of her clients.

Few saints have suffered less from calumny and misunderstanding than St Margaret of Scotland. Her exquisite tact, her perfect selflessness, and unwearying thought for others, together with her freedom from anything approaching self-righteousness, made everybody love her, and so she changed and renewed and improved at her will, without any of the friction that often attends innovations. Once, indeed, if tradition speaks truth, an evil tongue sought to injure the saintly Queen's reputation, and this was the only occasion of a shadow between husband and wife.

The incident occurred in the early days of St Margaret's married life, and at a time when Malcolm's carelessness about the needs of his soul occasioned his young wife considerable anxiety. It was not her way to weary him with reproaches, but she poured out her heart's desire to God in prayer, and punished her own innocent body by fasts and penances to win graces for her husband.

The forests around Dunfermline teemed with game—not only the mild varieties of our own day being there in abundance, but also the wolf and the ferocious wild boar. Hunting was a dangerous pastime, and probably because it was so, Malcolm loved it. If he could not be in the thick of battle, fighting against savage men, the next best thing was the pursuit of these savage beasts, and Queen Margaret sighed when she saw him set forth—anxious alike for the body and soul of this wild lord of hers. It was not part of her idea of wifely duty, however, to absent herself or look gloomy because her husband refused to be a stay-at-home to please her. When the hunting- party left the Castle, she was there with her ladies, smiling and beautiful, to wave a farewell, and Malcolm carried the memory of her fair face with him through all the wild deeds of the day.

As the last sounds of the hunt died away, the Queen was in the habit of dismissing her women. They went back to their needlework, and she, alone and thoughtful, wended her way down a steep woodland path to the dell, part of which is still preserved in the heart of busy Dunfermline. Here Nature had made her an oratory—a cave hewn out of the native rock by one or other of the disintegrating forces, and hidden in its recesses, she could give herself up undisturbed, to prayer and penance—a queen no longer, but simply a creature alone with her Creator.

The mischief-maker, a young man in the King's following, dared not make open accusations against the Queen, but imitating the cunning of Satan, whose work he was doing, he sought to poison Malcolm's mind gradually by suggestions and insinuations. He gently edged in a word from time to time until he got the King's mind to dwell on the difference between himself and his wife—he, middle-aged and uncouth—she, young and beautiful; he, a great rough soldier—she, refined and gentle; he, ignorant she, learned and accomplished. The tempter spoke pityingly and marvelled that a lady of so many graces could be content to dwell in dull Dunfermline. Malcolm bade the man be silent, but his not too even temper was ruffled and his peace of mind gone.

Not at all self-sufficient, the poor King easily owned to himself that Margaret might well desire more than he with all his loving goodwill could give her, and when at home again he found himself furtively studying her face, seeking in it traces of the discontent which he began to persuade himself must be there. He could not appreciate his own worth as his wife did, and was easily induced to lay too much stress on appearances.

Seeing evidence of his success in the King's preoccupation, the calumniator ventured to try again. One day, he remarked on the Queen's gay farewell, as the hunting-party left the Tower, and wondered if she

St Margaret's Cave

ever thought how easily the expedition might have a tragic ending, and then—it was but a suggestion—perhaps the Queen had amusements of her own in her lord's absence. It was said that she spent hours alone in the woods when he went a-hunting but ladies, young and lovely as she, were seldom so fond of solitude. The tone said more than the words, and Malcolm was wild with rage and jealousy, and yet angry with himself for being so much moved by mere words. What he said or did to his presuming follower we are not told, but he brooded on the evil import of what he had just heard, and grew more and more miserable. Yet he dissembled his feelings and bided his time, resolved to find out for himself how his wife spent her time in the forest dell.

One morning the hunting-party went out as usual, but presently Malcolm separated himself from the company and returned alone to the Tower. He was just in time to see the Queen with eyes bent thoughtfully on the ground slowly taking her solitary way along the woodland path. Silently he followed her, keeping at a distance and well in the shadow of the trees. Presently Queen Margaret, turning a sharp corner, disappeared suddenly, and the King, pausing a moment to grasp his sword, dashed after her. He found himself close to a miniature waterfall. The brook babbled as it tumbled over the rocks, just avoiding in its fall, the rock-hewn oratory of the Queen, and Malcolm heard the sweet tones of her voice mingled with the murmur of the cascade, and the music of the birds singing in the trees overhead. She was praying to God with all the loving abandonment that her supposed solitude warranted, and her prayer was for her husband that God would touch his brave, noble heart and lead him to realise the truth of the words:—

What does it profit a man if he gain the whole world and suffer the loss of his own soul.

Poor Malcolm! Struck with shame at the thought of his unworthy suspicions, he sank to the earth with a groan, and the clanking noise made by his sword on the pebbly ground brought the startled Queen from the cave where she had been prostrate in prayer. To her astonishment she found her husband prostrate outside, his face hidden in his hands and his whole being sunk in deepest self-abasement. She raised him up, heard his story, and forgave and comforted him like a naughty child, and doubtless she also won from him promises of fidelity to his spiritual duties in future. They went home together through the woods to the Tower, and the shadow was gone forever.

Several of St Margaret's books got a costly binding in the year that followed, and her oratory cave was furnished with the most beautiful appointments and ornaments that her generous husband could obtain for it. The Queen let him have his way, as she always did in such matters. Probably she would have preferred her retreat in all its pristine bareness, but new methods of mortification were easily found, and she would not hurt her dear penitent's feelings or prevent a generous act on his part for the sake of her own preferences. St Margaret's penances were never a reproach or an inconvenience to others. She kept the secrets of the King of kings as to His communications with her soul, and humbly believed that others had their secrets, too, knowing that God has different ways of leading souls to Himself. Thus she was hard and severe with herself, but always kind and considerate with regard to others.

Attentive to his religious duties at first chiefly to please his Queen, Malcolm soon began to find sweetness and comfort in them, and he enjoyed a peace such as he had never known before. It happened then that what he had begun to please St Margaret, he continued, to please God. Turgot, the Queen's confessor, cannot sufficiently express his admiration for the piety of this warlike king. "He learnt from her," says this chronicler, "to watch the night in prayer. I could not enough admire, to see the fervour of this prince at prayer, and to discover so much compunction of heart and such tears of devotion in a secular man."

Queen Margaret made great changes at Dunfermline. The hitherto bare walls of the Tower were covered with rich tapestries and beautiful hangings, securing privacy in some apartments and protection from the weather in others, for the masonry was none too compact. The Queen even procured a few panes of glass, very wonderful in the Scotland of the eleventh century, though certainly not beautiful or even very transparent; and we are told that these were carried between Dunfermline and Edinburgh, according to the residence of the royal family for the time being. The Queen herself wore rich and elegant garments, and she loved beauty and order in the appointments of all about her. Another royal saint, Queen Elizabeth of Hungary, distinguished herself by setting court usage aside and dressing like a peasant amid the splendours of a palace. In her day and at her court the sumptuousness of personal attire was in danger of being carried to excess, and the Queen's simplicity served as a check to such extravagance, reminding gay young people that they had souls to adorn as well as bodies.

With Queen Margaret of Scotland, circumstances were very different. Civilisation was in its infancy in her kingdom, and she found herself its nursing-mother. Her people were noble and brave as any she had known in other countries, but she would have them cultured, too; and culture and refinement were sadly wanting. The young Queen had to establish customs befitting royalty and to secure for it the dignity and consequence that would make it honoured and respected. She and her husband, indeed, with their regal personalities, might easily dispense with mere trappings of state, but there was the future to consider, and St Margaret sought to make things easier for those who would come after her. There were the people to consider also. The royal home was the highest in Scotland, and as to the city set on a hill, all eyes were turned to it. Humbler homes looked to it as the model, and the Queen would therefore make it a noble ideal—as beautiful and gracious as possible.

It was not enough that she should be a perfect wife and mother; she had to be a schoolmistress, too. Scotland was her school, and its people her pupils. The Scots had much to learn. It was but a few hundred years before, that their ancestors had roamed through their native forests, clad in the skins of animals and, needless to say, not too particular about picturesque dwellings and daintily appointed tables. Even in the eleventh century there were few houses of stone in Scotland and these were rudely built and more rudely furnished, while their owners, as a rule, were easily satisfied in the matter of food and clothing. Provided always that it was sufficient for their needs, appearance went for little. Innate nobility and natural refinement were not wanting. These ancient Scots were quick to recognise excellence of every kind and yield it admiration, but then, at such a distance from more civilised countries and living amid scenes of almost constant warfare, their opportunities were few.

Queen Margaret with her unerring knowledge of character realised at once what she had to do. Taste had to be trained and higher ideals of conduct and beauty had to be set before these grownup children. She expected appreciation and ready imitation, and she was right. Her methods were entirely successful, and gradually to the King's delight there gathered round his Queen a court circle, the politeness and refinement of whose members was not unworthy of its gracious centre. Nor was Queen Margaret unmindful of her husband's dignity.

He, too, had to dress in accordance with his rank, and to submit to be attended by a numerous and well-equipped retinue, whenever he went abroad. At home the number of his attendants was increased and he was waited on no longer by men of low birth but by the nobles, who soon came to consider it an honour to be so employed. At table Malcolm was served in gold and silver plate and had to be much more decorous in eating than formerly, and his apartments became so splendid that it was some time before he could accustom himself to their elegance. As to his public appearances—they were attended by pomp and ceremony previously unknown in Scotland and never failed to make a great sensation among the simple folk.

Thus St Margaret had something to teach everybody and yet there was nothing aggressive in her teaching, none of that arrogant assumption of Saxon superiority, which has so often wounded the susceptibilities of the Gaels in later intercourse between the two countries.

St Margaret's gentle tact is well exemplified in the story of the "Grace Cup." At her first banquets she was considerably disturbed in mind by the behaviour of the rough Scottish nobles. They were accustomed to consult their own inclinations only, and as soon as their appetites were appeased they rushed from the table with scant ceremony and no consideration for the presence of either Queen or chaplain. The latter *"said grace"*—the phrase was the same then as now—but few of the male guests were ever left to join in the thanksgiving. Queen Margaret neither remonstrated nor showed displeasure, but she quietly made up her mind that God should be honoured by a grace in which all who had partaken of the meal should join, and also that her banquets should not be broken up with such unseemly haste and rudeness.

One day she smilingly invited her guests to remain to the end of the feast. After grace, she told them, a cup of choicest wine from her own table would be sent to each and it was her desire that they should drink it in her honour. Who could refuse such a flattering invitation? Nobody left the board before grace that day, and as the favour became a custom at subsequent banquets, the Queen had no more cause for complaint. For centuries after St Margaret's death the grace-cup followed every Scottish feast, and it would have been a grave mark of discourtesy to refuse to drink of it.

Gradually the primitive manners of the Scottish court gave place to pomp and state similar to that of the royalty of England and continental countries. Communication with other lands became frequent and trade and commerce began to flourish in consequence. Merchants came from all parts of the Continent and found ready purchasers for their wares among the aspiring Scots.

St Margaret never learnt to speak Gaelic well, and by degrees the language spoken south of the Forth and Clyde—mainly Saxon and the ancestor of what we now call "broad Scots"—became the ordinary court language. The majority of the people of Scotland continued to use the Gaelic language for hundreds of years after St Margaret's time, but the court never returned to it again. "Broad Scots" is, unhappily, dying out or sinking to the level of a mere dialect, but until the beginning of the nineteenth century and its easy intercourse with England it was the language of all in Scotland—gentle and simple alike—who did not speak Gaelic. It is more Saxon by far than the English language itself, which, besides being saturated with Norman words, as a result of the Conquest, is a borrower from every other language on the face of the earth.

CHAPTER 5

Margaret, Protectress of the Poor

Though nearly nine centuries have passed since Queen Margaret kept house in Dunfermline Tower or on Edinburgh's rugged rock and sent the rays of her sunny influence far and near over the "land of brown heath and shaggy wood," we know fairly well how her days were spent. They were busy days, and if the good Queen wore gorgeous raiment, she certainly gave but scant time to the consideration of it or of anything personal, except, indeed, that most important of all personal possessions, her own soul. Early in her married life, distrustful of herself and believing, like the true daughter of the Church that she always was, that it is better, at least in spiritual things, to be guided by another than by oneself, she looked around for a worthy priest who would be at once her confessor and her spiritual director.

People spoke much of the sanctity and learning of Turgot, Prior of St Andrew's and formerly of St Cuthbert's Monastery, Durham, and the Queen obtained from her husband the favour of having this holy man appointed chaplain of the royal palace. She put herself at once under Turgot 's spiritual direction and followed his rules for the guidance of her soul with perfect obedience. It is from his chronicle, written at the request of St Margaret's daughter, Matilda Queen of England, that we know something of his saintly penitent's inner life and also most of the details concerning her prayer and works of charity. As to her penances he often desired the Queen to moderate them, though he dared not altogether forbid what was so evidently a great means of sanctification. It was only at the last, when St Margaret was ill and suffering, and death was drawing near, that she could be prevailed upon to give up some of her beloved penitential exercises.

The enthusiastic admiration with which this "soul's friend" of the good Queen speaks of her life, gives the reader a high idea of the hidden sanctity, of which, as her confessor, he may not speak so freely. "Every action," he tells us, "was distinguished by moderation and gentleness. When she spoke, her conversation was seasoned with the salt of wisdom; when she was silent, her silence was full of good thoughts."

Good thoughts hidden deep in the fertile soil of a pure heart are the seeds from which spring the flowers and fruits of kind words and good deeds, and St Margaret's heart must have been well planted with such seeds, for her life was a veritable garden of these flowers and fruits. She gave her means and her energies in generous measure for the spiritual and temporal welfare of the poor and the sick, and especially of the children, not with the altruistic motives of modern philanthropists, but just because these unfortunates were Christ's little ones "and in ministering to them she was ministering to Him, for had He not said '*Whatsoever you shall do to these, my least brethren, you shall do it unto Me*'?"

"She was poorer than any of her paupers," says her biographer, "for they, even when they had nothing, wished to have something, while all her anxiety was to strip herself of what she had." Queen Margaret was an early riser winter and summer alike, and winter mornings were dismal and cold, even in a palace, in those primitive days. The feeble light of a candle made the darkness visible and the fire of wood or turf—if it was lit so early—served only to make the unheated chapel colder by contrast. Each morning the Queen spent several hours in her chapel. There were long private prayers while the rest of the household were still asleep and during this time "only her body was here below, for her spirit was near to God." Several low Masses were generally said very early in the royal chapel and all these St Margaret heard with the greatest devotion, being still on her knees when the household assembled for the daily High Mass.

Every day of the year the good Queen waited on twenty-four poor people at their first meal before she broke her own fast. This number of pensioners she supported always, and when good fortune or death made a break in their ranks, the vacant place was at once filled by another needy one, always easily found. All her life, St Margaret had these favoured poor folks near her, for when she removed from one residence to another, she insisted that they should accompany her and their morning meal was always her own especial care. "Not until after she had devoutly waited upon Christ in these His poor, was it her habit to refresh her own feeble body." The good Queen's ordinary days were full of charity, but during the forty days preceding Christmas, and the forty days of Lent, it seemed as if her desires could not be satisfied and she multiplied her prayers and good works to such an extent that people wondered how she found time for her multitudinous secular duties.

During these holy seasons she spent the greater part of every night in prayer. In the evening she retired for a short rest, but was up and in the chapel before midnight. It was her custom to say the divine office at this time and also the offices of the dead, and the *Psalter*. When the office of *matins* and lands, sung by the priests, was finished, she returned to her chamber and washed the feet of six poor persons whom she found waiting. It was one of the chamberlain's duties to have these people in the house overnight, that the Queen might satisfy her desire for charity, and they always returned home blessing her, no less for her loving kindness than for the generous alms which accompanied it. Her act of charity over, St Margaret would go to bed and take some much-needed rest, but it was brief, for there were works of mercy yet to be done and prayers to be said before the commencement of the first Mass.

Nine little orphans were brought up at the Queen's expense and these she cared for herself throughout the penitential seasons. They were brought to her at an early hour and she loved to wash and dress and feed them, taking the very little ones on her knee as tenderly as if they had been her own children and feeding them with the spoon she used herself. The frequent wars made orphans numerous enough and it was always one of St Margaret's favourite charities to provide for these helpless children. In hundreds of Scottish homes in the years to come, the good wife would gather the "bairns" round her knee in the "ingle-neuk" and tell them tales of her childhood in the royal palace and of the care and kindness of the good Queen who had been as a mother to her and many others, orphaned by the ravages of war or fell disease.

With grateful pride St Margaret's words of kindly counsel would be repeated, and her lessons given over again—lessons in cleanliness—and care of the body as well as of the soul—for though the Queen had such tenderness and commiseration for poverty, she had none for dirt, and saw no reason why the two should go hand-in-hand in a country like Scotland, where water was so pure and abundant. Thus it was that she spoke to future generations as well as to her own and her apostolate continued for centuries after her loving heart had ceased to beat and her once busy hands were still.

After the orphans had been fed and tended, the King joined his wife, and together they went to the royal hall where attendants had already assembled some three hundred poor people. These were arranged in order round the great room and when the King and Queen had entered, the doors were shut, for none were allowed to be present at this almsgiving except the chaplain and a few attendants. Both Malcolm and Margaret waited on these lowly guests, serving them with food and drink, and speaking words of help and encouragement that were even more strengthening. Many men and women, who had found life's problems too numerous and too difficult and were tempted in consequence to despair and give up the contest, came forth from the royal presence with fresh vigour and with fortitude enough for a resolution to take a new standpoint and try again.

When all her poor guests had been attended to, the Queen repaired to chapel or church and poured out her heart in prayer to God for all those depending on her. Sometimes she heard as many as five or six low Masses before the household assembled for High Mass. Silent and motionless, she knelt hour after hour, offering herself as a sacrifice to God and praying with such fervour and earnestness that the tears streamed from her eyes. Let those who think her victories easily won, contemplate her here before the altar in closest union with her Lord and Master, and consider how powerful is the prayer of a pure and humble heart! If we could pray as St Margaret did, we too, like her should "speak of victory."

When High Mass was over it was time for the Queen's own repast, but before she partook of it there were still her twenty-four pensioners to be served and waited on. It was not far from midday when at last she broke her fast and then her meal was ascetic in the extreme. She was always abstemious, so much so that her ordinary meals were like the fasts of other people, but during penitential seasons and in times of war and consequent anxiety, she seemed scarcely to eat at all. At meals taken in company with others, she was careful to hide her mortifications. By agreeable conversation and attention to the needs of others, which was, of course, her duty as hostess, she cleverly avoided notice with regard to her own easily satisfied requirements, and she was always less abstemious at the household table than when she was served privately.

At times of anxiety when the King was engaged in important state affairs, or absent on one of his frequent warlike expeditions to the north or south, St Margaret spent extra hours before the altar or in her cave oratory, interceding with sighs and tears for husband, children, and people. In addition to all this, every season had its own appropriate prayers, and the Queen never wearied or thought she had done enough. In Lent she said the entire *Psalter* three or four times a day, and then, too, she multiplied her penances and, as we have seen, her acts of charity and mercy.

The Queen . . .
Oftener on her knees than on her feet,
Died every day she lived.

This by a strange mistake is what Shakespeare says of Malcolm's mother, though there is no doubt that it was Malcolm's wife that he was really thinking of when he wrote the words. But it was not only while on her knees that the good Queen prayed. She lived always in God's Presence and so her life was a continual prayer. That strong will of hers was used in the first place to conquer self, and hence its marvellous influence over others. They who would teach others must first be learners and they only can rule well, who have learnt to obey.

Before, but more especially after, St Margaret's death, wonderful stories were told of her power with God. Great numbers were sometimes fed from a store which, humanly speaking, was all inadequate, and money seemed to multiply in the good Queen's hands, when she had slaves to ransom or poor men's debts to pay. The touch of the same gentle hands, as St Margaret dressed the wounds of her suffering poor, often brought relief and healing, and the cure was gratefully ascribed to the hand rather than to the ointment and dressing.

St Margaret's humility was so well known that none dared speak aloud of these marvels; but they tenderly whispered them to each other and to their children as they gave thanks to God. It was no wonder to them that He should bestow more than earthly power on one who loved and served Him so well as did their beloved Queen.

Turgot has evidently heard the stories told by the people and probably he could tell many more wonderful, himself, but he respects the Queen's secrets after her death as he had done in her lifetime, and his chronicle tells of no wonders connected with her charities. "Others," he says, "may admire the indications of sanctity which miracles afford; I admire much more the works of mercy which I perceived in Margaret. Miracles are common to the evil and the good but the works of true piety and charity are peculiar to the good." Yet he would have us know that he has not told us everything about his saintly penitent.

Addressing her daughter Queen Matilda, for whom his chronicle is written, he says:—

It is my wish that you should know and others through you, that were I to attempt to recount all I could tell to her honour, I might be suspected, while praising your mother to be really flattering your queenly dignity. . . . I suppress many things fearing that they might appear incredible.

Throughout Fife, and in Edinburgh, too, there were many legends about "Sweet St Margaret" in Catholic ages. Such stories are at least founded on truth and certainly those relating to the good Queen show how she lived in the hearts of her people and how all-powerful they considered her to be with God, for whose sake she was so good to them and to their children. The following is a Fifeshire legend, one of many often told at the firesides of "the kingdom" before the Reformation.

St Margaret had found a weeping, disconsolate mother standing by the door of a rude dwelling in the wood. Her child was within, ill dying perhaps, and she had nothing to give him, neither food nor medicine. The illness was infectious—the plague it might be—and the terrified neighbours fled at the poor mother's approach, leaving her quite alone in her trouble. She told the Queen between her sobs that none would enter her cottage, but St Margaret had no fear for herself and went in without any hesitation. She soothed the child and comforted the mother and left them both comparatively happy, promising to send help at once and also plenty of food and medicine.

At the Tower she found all she wanted except a messenger, for rumours of the infected hut in the wood had gone abroad and everybody shrank back in horror at the thought of approaching it. The Queen would not force even a slave into a position of danger, but there was at least one person over whom she had entire control and who never shirked a duty because it was disagreeable or dangerous. Not for the first time she was her own messenger, setting out alone on her errand of mercy, with the heavy basket of provisions hidden by her cloak.

As she descended the incline St Margaret saw, coming to meet her, King Malcolm, accompanied by a stranger, evidently a new arrival from the south, for the Conquest sent many Saxon nobles to seek hospitality at the Scottish Court. The Queen went on but drew her cloak closer, to cover more completely the burden which she carried.

Malcolm guessed that she was on some charitable errand, and nothing loth to give his guest an example of his sweet wife's goodness, he playfully asked what she carried in the folds of her cloak. "Woodland flowers, perhaps," he said, with a smile of superior knowledge, while his courteous companion hastened to improve the occasion by telling him that the Queen herself was the fairest flower of the woodland. Malcolm's hand was on her cloak and she breathed a prayer to our Lord that He would help her. Her charities were His secrets and in her humility she would fain escape human praise. It was but an instant—the folds of the mantle were gently drawn aside and lo! there was revealed a basket filled with fresh woodland flowers.

Canmore and his friend took leave of the Queen and passed on to the Tower, while St Margaret pursued her way to the cottage and the sick child. The poor mother found something more substantial than wild flowers in the basket and the good Queen left her comforted and grateful and full of hope for the future. Meanwhile, the King had been apprised of the purpose of St Margaret's walk in the woods for her attendants were already ashamed of their cowardice. He kept his own counsel when he heard of the Queen's burden, but he was very serious and thoughtful when she returned and his eyes glowed with love and veneration as often as they rested on her fair face with its halo of golden hair. Is the story true? We do not know. It easily may be, for God's Hand was not shortened by the passing of eleven centuries. The same power that could change water into wine at Cana could change food into wild flowers and wild flowers into food again at Dunfermline if Christ so willed.

CHAPTER 6

Margaret, Queen of Scotland

St Margaret's prayers and works of mercy filled so much of her day that there would appear room for little else, but her secular duties were certainly not neglected. When we read of them first, we wonder how the good Queen found any time for prayer. Household business alone was considerable where there was so much teaching and training to be done. Habits of order and even of cleanliness had to be acquired by St Margaret's domestics, and it was not the work of a day to make her staff realise what she expected of them. It is easy to tell in a few words that she effected a transformation at court, the civilising and refining influence of which went out wave after wave, over the length and breadth of Scotland, but the transition period must have been a time of arduous labour, thoughtful planning and constant tact.

The work was not accomplished either, by the mere giving of orders. Those who teach and train others must be capable of giving object lessons and showing that what they require, can be done. As time went on the Queen procured helpers from England and other parts of Europe, and less actual work was needed on her own part, but all her life she accustomed herself to daily tasks of lowly helpfulness. These humble deeds never took from her dignity, but they acquired dignity of their own because she did them. Every womanly act of hers was a queenly act in the highest sense.

Besides her orphanage and poor people, St Margaret had a hospital under her roof into which she gathered all the infirm poor who could not be treated properly in their own wretched homes. Many of her patients, owing to neglect and dirt, were covered with loathsome sores and horrible diseases of the skin, and these were the good Queen's favourites. She would dress their wounds herself with wonderful gentleness and tenderness, kissing the foul sores as she cleansed and bound them up. It was easy for the poor sufferers to believe in the loving goodness and mercy of God when they saw this beautiful earthly Queen moving about among them like an angel of love and mercy.

Very early in their married life Queen Margaret began to advise and help her husband in the government of his kingdom, and its consolidation was as much due to her tact as to his vigour, for men yielded to her gentle persuasion, when they would have resisted to the death, at Malcolm's stern demand. During the King's frequent absences on war intent, all looked to the good Queen for guidance and help and it was part of her daily business to hear petitions and complaints from every part of the country. In order that access to her might be easier, St Margaret frequently sat in an open field that all might be encouraged to approach and speak freely. An eighteenth century life tells us that according to constant tradition, the stone by which she rested when she first came to Dunfermline, was her favourite seat of justice. St Margaret's Stone is rather more than a mile from Dunfermline Tower, but the good Queen walked and rode many a mile in the cause of justice and mercy.

Law-making in Scotland was yet primitive in Canmore's time, and when laws were made they were often of little avail owing to faulty administration. Wrongs, real or imaginary, were numerous, and who was to settle disputes and assign blame and punishment to the guilty? Sometimes public officials were in fault, sometimes private individuals, but the only chance of redress lay in petitioning the King. Malcolm put all these matters into St Margaret's hands, and oftentimes she spent several hours of the day hearing the grievances of the poor. An artist might find in the scene a fitting subject for a picture: the background of hill and forest and picturesque Tower, and the green slopes near Dunfermline, peopled for the time being, from the great stone to the silver sea far below, with all who had tales of want and wrong to tell. The setting would be worthy of its central figure—the beautiful fair-haired Queen, resplendent in her shining robes, seated on her rocky throne and bending low to listen with tender pity to a story of misery and suffering.

St Margaret employed agents of ability and fidelity in this business, sending them all over Scotland to inquire into cases of distress that had been reported to her, and to report on others which they might discover while on their rounds. It was their duty to see that the Queen's instructions were carried out and effect given to her judgments.

The work was good in itself, but it was more important still as a foundation on which others could build. David I., St Margaret's wise and saintly son, improved very considerably on her methods when he came to the throne. He appointed a judge or sheriff over each county whose duty it was to decide all cases in the King's name. David himself, however, was always ready, as his mother had been, to give personal attention to the complaints and petitions of the lowly ones of his kingdom. He was in the habit of sitting at his palace gates on certain days that he might hear their cases and deal justly with them; and he considered it no indignity when a royal progress was interrupted in order that some importunate old dame might pour out the tale of her woes to the "protector of the poor."

Slavery was the greatest curse of Scotland in the eleventh century and for a long time after it. We can only with difficulty think of our ancestors either as slaves or as slave-owners. The desire of freedom for self and others—the love of independence—is such an integral part of Scottish character as we know it, that the thing seems impossible. It is only too true, however. The evil began in savage and pagan times when the motto was "*Woe to the vanquished*," and all who were on the losing side in fight or foray expected death or bondage as a natural consequence of defeat.

Christianity was everywhere the determined enemy of slavery, and as the Church grew more powerful in any country, slaves and slave-owners became fewer in number. St Columba and his followers had preached freedom, but when the Danes came, that and many other precepts of the Scottish apostles were forgotten. St Margaret did much to alleviate the miseries caused by slavery but she was powerless to abolish it altogether. Indeed, her fierce husband never went to war without swelling the ranks of the unfortunate slaves by bringing home a train of captives. Poor Queen Margaret! She could only try to help the wretched sufferers and pray and hope for better times. What now of the wife's wishes being a law to her husband? Ah! This was an evil of long standing and could not be swept away in a day at the word of a gentle woman. The good Queen was prudent and patient and did not expect impossibilities, but she did what she could in the present and made plans for the future. St Margaret was always willing to sow, in order that others might reap. Her desire was that good should be done, not merely that she herself might do it.

Her pity for the poor slaves was intense and she spent large sums of money in ransoming them. Her agents were encouraged to bring her news of any specially hard cases and when she heard of one, she never rested until she found some means of relieving the pool creature's misery. The time was not ripe for great changes, but she could help individual cases and spread abroad a feeling of kindly sympathy for the hard fate of poor slaves. Perhaps—for St Margaret had occasional glimpses of the future—she may have been comforted and encouraged by a foreknowledge of the better state of things that her own reforms would gradually bring about.

Through St Margaret's efforts, and those of her children, the Church became a power in the land, and as religion spread abroad, slavery declined. It was not, however, until after the wars of Scottish Independence in the thirteenth and fourteenth centuries that serfdom, as it was called, ceased to exist. Many slaves obtained their freedom for services rendered to their country during the war, and others fled to the towns in the frequent periods of confusion. They became free if they could elude the vigilance of their late masters for a year and a day; and it was comparatively easy to do so; for search was difficult and the escaped slave could always count on the sympathy and help of neighbours.

When Scotland settled down to something like peace, after the Battle of Bannockburn, serfdom was discredited and dying, and, chiefly owing to the determined efforts of the Church, there was scarcely a trace of it left at the beginning of the fifteenth century.

External work never took Queen Margaret's attention from the "sweet ordering" of her own household. She had to form a court for herself and soon gathered around her some of the noblest matrons and maidens in Scotland. It was a new and wonderful experience for the chosen ones, for they were the first ladies-in-waiting to grace a Scottish court. The Queen was strict with her women and took care that they had plenty of occupation. She taught them needlework and embroidery, and under her supervision they made exquisite vestments for use in Dunfermline and other churches.

Until the Reformation, work of this kind was at once the chief occupation and recreation of both English and Scottish ladies. It was a labour of love, and while the fingers were active, in order that God might be honoured more becomingly, the hearts of the workers were drawn closer to Him.

Ye lovely ladyes
With youre longe fyngres
That ye have silk and sandel
To sowe when tyme is

St Margaret encouraged innocent mirth and gaiety among her "lovely ladyes" while they plied the needle with their "longe fyngres," but she could not tolerate levity or frivolity. The chronicler tells us that "in her presence nothing unseemly was ever done or uttered." Yet it does not appear that the royal lady used any stronger measures to secure this good behaviour than her own example and the sweet strength of character which made her mere presence a compelling force for good. "The Queen," says Turgot, "united so much strictness with her sweetness of temper, so great pleasantness even with her severity that all who waited upon her—men as well as women—loved her, while they feared her, and in fearing, loved her."

St Margaret's maids of honour were especially devoted to her and evidently as eager to learn as their mistress was to teach. Her reforms met with remarkably little opposition or criticism from any quarter, but there seems to have been none at all from womankind. The good Queen claimed and obtained for women of every degree a position of honour and respect, such as had not been known in Scotland until her coming; and opened out before their astonished and delighted eyes new possibilities of usefulness and happiness and goodness. They on their part admired and loved their royal mistress. Many esteemed her a saint and revered her accordingly, and all were glad and willing to have their ideals of life raised and ennobled. No jealousy appears to have interfered in any way with the Queen's household reforms.

As time went on Queen Margaret became the mother of six sons and two daughters, and the care of these royal children was not the lightest of her many burdens. King Malcolm, occupied with a thousand duties of state, left his wife to order the young lives of their children and make such arrangements regarding education as she thought fit. He knew that this important matter was safe in the hands of his saintly Queen.

Tutors were engaged for the young princes as soon as they were old enough to profit by continuous teaching, and St Margaret took care that these should be men of piety as well as of learning. The two princesses were taught for the most part by the Queen herself, and she carefully supervised the religious instruction of all her children. Some writers lay stress on her strictness, but the royal children seem to have thriven on it. They loved their mother devotedly while she lived, and after her death they reverenced her as a saint.

Convinced as St Margaret was of the necessity of "dying daily" there was naturally no foolish fondness or indulgence about her methods. She would have her boys—yes, and her girls—able to conquer and control themselves and to do their duty readily, courageously and cheerfully, even when it was not agreeable. "Teach them above all things to love and fear God" was her parting injunction to the Confessor she trusted most, and this was always her own most important lesson for her children.

Results speak for themselves. St Margaret's sons and daughters grew up around her to be the pride and hope of Scotland. She did not live to see how nobly they fulfilled the fair promise of childhood, but the story of their lives is the best eulogy on her training.

They were for the most part distinguished by intellect and accomplishments, and both princesses were beautiful and made brilliant marriages. High, however, as many of them were placed in the world when they reached manhood and womanhood, they are more celebrated for goodness than for greatness, and this is just what their saintly mother desired for them. It was no hard and severe training in virtue that made a whole family delight in it all their lives as did these princes and princesses. St Margaret had taught them her own secret of serving God for love.

In after years three of St Margaret's sons became in turn kings of Scotland and they were among her best and ablest rulers. "No history," says William of Malmesbury, "has recorded three kings and brothers who were of equal sanctity and savoured so much of their mother's piety." David I. especially did great things for his country. With all his mother's zeal for the beauty of God's House, he covered Scotland with fine churches, including those of Holy rood, Melrose and Jedburgh. He encouraged learning and desired that boys of every degree in life should frequent the monastery schools even though they were not destined for the priesthood. He improved trade and commerce and made good laws, but better still, he made arrangements to secure that old laws should be better kept.

In his day "the key could keep the castle, an' the bracken bush the coo," and that was a good deal in those wild times. The first James of Scotland, the Poet-King, who lost his life through his zeal in trying to get similar order in his own day, said of David that he was "a sair sanct for the Croon." Poor James, with his almost empty treasury, the result of his long exile in England, thought wistfully of the money that his pious ancestor had spent in church-building. All the same the words were said more for the sake of their wit than for the thought they expressed, for James I. was clever enough to see and appreciate King David's work. He had continued St Margaret's system of reform and construction, and besides being a saint, he was a good friend to Scotland, and one of the best kings who ever sat on a Scottish throne.

CHAPTER 7

Margaret and Edinburgh

Malcolm Canmore was the first king of Scotland to use Edinburgh Castle as a royal residence and most writers give the credit of the wisdom and foresight of his choice to Queen Margaret. The great strength of the fortress on the rock, no less than its position in the valley between the two main parts of his kingdom, made Edinburgh an ideal station for such a monarch as Malcolm whose chief work was to unite the Celts of the north and the Saxons of the south into one compact Scottish people.

Edinburgh Castle stands on a magnificent rock 443 feet above the level of the sea and history does not reach backwards to a time when it did not exist in some form. In the misty ages of the past it was the abode of primitive princesses, daughters of Pictish kings. They were placed in this fortress for safety in those wild days and many of them never left it, but spent their entire lives in solitary state—of a kind—probably bewailing the elevation, literal as well as metaphorical, which condemned them to such isolation.

In the seventh century the Northumbrian Edwin forced the stronghold out of the hands of the Picts, and strengthened its fortifications to suit his own requirements. Even in his day it was called the Maidens' Castle (*Castrum puellarum*), and it does not seem clear whether the name Edinburgh, given to the cluster of habitations which soon began to grow more and more visible on the only sloping ridge of the rock, is a corruption of Edwin's Burgh or of Maidens' Burgh.

The Maidens' Castle in the eleventh century was surrounded by dense forests broken in parts by rising ground covered with gorse; and the crests of green hills met the southern skies then as now. In the forest land, wild beasts unknown in our modern Scottish woods, roamed about in considerable numbers. There were wolves and boars

EDINBURGH CASTLE

and great white bulls, the descendants, perhaps, of some of the flower-bedecked victims slaughtered of old by the Druids in their sacrifices. At an earlier period there were bears also in the woods of Caledonia, but probably the last of the race had died out before the days of St Margaret.

The district was, and is, well-watered. Streams are numerous though there is no river of great importance nearer than the Forth, and in the hollow which is now the beautiful West Princes Street Gardens, there was an extensive sheet of water known for centuries as the Nor' Loch.

For two years after their marriage Malcolm Canmore and his queen lived almost entirely at Dunfermline, and their eldest son was born in the Tower. In 1072 they went to Edinburgh for the first time and after this date the Castle became a frequently inhabited residence, though the royal family always loved Dunfermline and generally spent some part of the year there. Queen Margaret's sister, the Princess Christina, soon returned to England to enter a convent as she had always desired to do, but Edgar the Atheling, as he continued to be called, remained at the Scottish court much longer. He hoped against hope that with Malcolm's assistance he would at last ascend the English throne, just as Malcolm had mounted the Scottish throne with English aid. Malcolm did his best for the realisation of his brother-in-law's hopes, but the odds against poor Edgar were too great, and it began to be evident that the Normans had come to stay.

The Scottish king twice gave Edgar Atheling a princely outfit, including "golden and silver vessels" and at last he persuaded him to give up his hopeless pretensions to the throne of England and submit to William. How readily the Conqueror made friends with his weak rival appears from the fact that we soon hear of Edgar as using his influence with the Normans to procure easier terms for his brother-in-law, brought to bay at Abernethy; and later as being in a position to befriend his orphaned nephews and nieces. The Atheling appears to have taken part in the Crusade with Robert of Normandy at a later period, but misfortune attended him in that as in most of his enterprises, and his end is hidden in obscurity.

When St Margaret first went to Edinburgh there was small promise of its developing into the beautiful city that is "Scotia's darling seat" today. It consisted of a few habitations on the eastern slope of the rock—wretched huts, most of them—with walls of wattle and roofs thatched with heather. Two little churches were similarly constructed—St Cuthbert's, close to the rock and St Giles' at the edge of the forest. The names remain, but the faith of the worshippers has changed.

Neither St Cuthbert's nor St Giles' was convenient for Queen Margaret with her ever growing court and her colony of Saxon refugees, and she had a third small church built for herself on the summit of the crag. Stone instead of wattle was used in its construction, and, though nearly nine hundred years old, it is still in a state of excellent preservation. Some say that the little building is complete, and others, that it is only a fragment of a larger church.

In all probability we shall never know which view is the correct one. St Margaret's Chapel is the name by which it was known before the Reformation and by which it is again known in twentieth century and its earlier dedication in the Saint's lifetime is forgotten. It may have been St Margaret's then also for the good Queen had a tender devotion to her own name-saint and patron, St Margaret, the virgin-martyr of France.

After the change of religion in Scotland, St Margaret's Chapel was put to base uses, and its antiquity and former glory were forgotten. About the year 1850 it was discovered by some members of the Antiquarian Society and declared to be a treasure. The garrison had been using it as a store-house for ammunition, but a transformation was soon effected. By command of Queen Victoria, the oratory was restored in 1853 and it is now one of the chief objects of interest on the Castle Hill.

The three small windows are filled with stained glass, one representing St Margaret and the other two, Malcolm Canmore and St David, King of Scotland, the youngest son of Malcolm and Margaret.

An ancient legend tells that in this chapel St Margaret was favoured with one of the wonderful glimpses into the future with which God seems to have gifted her on several occasions. She saw how the beloved country of her adoption would have to suffer from England in the centuries to come, and she also saw its final triumph when her own descendants would secure its independence. On the wall of the chapel after this marvellous experience, she caused a painting to be made of a man scaling a rock and under the picture she had the words inscribed "*Gardez-vous Francois.*"

In 1312 when Robert the Bruce began his work of recovering the Scottish castles from English hands, it was a man named Francis who led Randolph and his party of picked men up the face of the cliff to surprise the English garrison. The story has often been told of Randolph's ambition to take Edinburgh Castle and of the coming of Francis with his daring plan. He had lived in the Castle as a boy, he told Randolph, and had often used the rock as a means of exit and entrance, to elude the vigilance of a too strict father. It seemed a rash adventure and it might easily be a trap, but "*nothing venture, nothing win*," and Randolph listened and resolved to try it. He could but die in the service of his country and Randolph would gladly have given his life to set Scotland free. He was himself a descendant of St Margaret for his mother was the sister of Robert the Bruce.

As the gallant party crept up the cliff on hands and knees and in single file they were nearly undone. An English soldier on duty above was bidding a friend good night and seeking to scare him, in rude pleasantry he threw a stone down the rock, at the same time exclaiming "Ha! I see you there." The stone struck several of the brave Scots as it bounded down the cliff and if one had made a movement all would have found their death then and there. But they remained silent and still, as the masses of rock around them and the friendly darkness concealed them, for it was night. With a loud laugh at his own joke the English soldier passed on but he was to laugh no more.

Randolph's attack was entirely successful and Bruce, with Edinburgh Castle his own, was encouraged to continue the struggle which ended so gloriously two years later, on the field of Bannockburn. St Margaret's prediction was still remembered in 1312, and people looked on the feat of Francis as its accomplishment, and reminded each other that Randolph, the hero, was of their dear Saint's kith and kin.

Saxons came in great numbers to the Scottish court during the first troubled years of the Conqueror's reign. They found a warm friend in Malcolm Canmore, who remembered his own exile and the kindness shown to him in England, and the Queen, of course, was their countrywoman and had fled as they were doing from Norman tyranny. Many of the English nobles, weary of the struggle and unable to bend their wills and submit to the arrogance of their foreign rulers, were ready to cast in their lot for good with their northern friends; and to these the Scottish king gave large grants of land in the south and east of Scotland. Some of our most important Lowland families owe their foundation to these Saxon exiles. Among them are the houses of Lyndesay, Vaux, Crichton, Maxwell, Leslie and Borthwick, all of which were established in Scotland in the reign of Malcolm Canmore and St Margaret.

There were other refugees, too, men and women of lower degree, who came north in the following of those who had been their lords in happier times. These were skilled in various crafts and industries, and the good Queen, ever on the alert to benefit her people, set the strangers to work to teach others what they themselves had learnt. This was the origin of more than one Scottish industry, and notably that of the linen manufacture of Dunfermline, Queen Margaret's favourite home.

The Queen encouraged learning also, and she found among her exiles many capable men and women who were eager to help her in her good work. Thus she made use of every opportunity of improving the condition of her people, and slowly but surely the work of civilisation went on. It is believed that St Margaret built a palace as well as a chapel on the Castle rock, but the great buildings of her sons and of her later descendants, the Stewart kings, make it impossible to identify any of the parts existing at her time, if, indeed, any still remain.

Several of St Margaret's children were born in Edinburgh, and the work of their education was partly carried on there. As at Dunfermline St Margaret had her orphans, her sick and her poor, and as soon as her daughters were old enough she associated them with her in her works of mercy. "When health and beauty were hers," says an ancient chronicler, "she devoted her strength to serve the poor uncultivated people whom God had committed to her care" and this was always her work of predilection. The service of the poor was evidently made no hard task to the little princesses. They were taught to love it and hold it in honour for Christ's sake as their holy mother herself did, and, young as they were when they lost her, they remembered and profited by the lessons she had given them. "The good Queen Maud," as the English people named the elder princess, when many years later she was their honoured queen, was only second to St Margaret herself in queenly works of charity and mercy.

The forests around Edinburgh Castle gradually disappeared as the trees were cut down to make way for more dwellings, and among the people of the little hamlet the good Queen was well known. She was the angel of mercy who brought help in time of need and who was ever ready with sympathy and kindly words to make affliction endurable. She helped the poor to live and made life nobler and brighter for them. In their sickness she tended them and taught them how to die, and often she was there at the deathbed, however lowly, to close the eyes of the dead and to comfort those left mourning. For hundreds of years after St Margaret's own happy death, "the good Queen" was a household word among the people of Scotland.

Queen Margaret had a great devotion to St Catherine of Alexandria, and a story in connection with it has come down to us. After St Catherine's martyrdom, her sacred body remained in Egypt until the eighth century. It was then discovered by the Christians and after a time was translated to the great monastery built by St Helen on Mount Sinai. The relics were greatly treasured by the monks, as was also a quantity of miraculous oil in some way connected with them. Queen Margaret had heard of this oil and was so desirous of possessing some of it that she earnestly besought St Catherine to make it possible. The legend tells how her prayer was granted. Queen Margaret was assured by St Catherine that God had given her the favour asked for, and that a messenger also named Catherine, was already on her way to Scotland with the oil.

After many perils by land and sea, this Catherine at length reached Liberton, and stood on its green heights to look on St Margaret's home, the goal of her toilsome journey.

Her heart swelled with emotion and forgetting her precious charge she suddenly threw out both her arms towards the Castle on the rock. Crash! The vessel lay in fragments on the stony ground and the oil was fast disappearing in the earth. Catherine fell on her knees in an agony of self-reproach and watched the thirsty soil drinking in her treasure. Lo! As she gazed a spring burst forth from the spot and oil was floating on its limpid water. So it floated when St Margaret came from Edinburgh Castle to look at it, and so it floats still, (at time of first publication). Anyone may see it who cares to visit the Balm Well of St Catherine at Liberton.

Crowds of sufferers visited St Catherine's Well in the centuries before the Reformation, and marvellous tales were told of cures effected there. The pious pilgrim from Mount Sinai seems to have spent the remainder of her life near the miraculous well, and a mound in the neighbourhood was long pointed out as St Catherine's grave.

Queen Margaret and her children often visited the Balm Well, and later sovereigns of Scotland did so for her sake. One of the Stewart kings erected a beautiful chapel on the height, and dedicated it to his saintly ancestress. This "St Margaret's Chapel," with many other treasures of a like kind, was destroyed at the Reformation.

James VI. of Scotland, however, loved St Catherine's Well and believed in its healing powers, and, when he came to Scotland after his accession to the English throne, he visited Liberton to drink again of its waters. Touched by the neglected appearance of the well, he had it railed in and repaired in honour of St Margaret, and it remains now probably much the same as when he last saw it. There are those living in the twentieth century who have found relief from pain by drinking of the waters of St Catherine's Well. It is our Scottish faith, and not St Margaret's oil, that has grown weak with the passing centuries.

Two fountains in Edinburgh bear the name of St Margaret's Well. One is in the Gardens near the Castle, and the other in the King's Park, south of Holy rood Palace. Near this second well, with Arthur's Seat high above it and the ruins of St Anthony's Chapel on the slope which forms one of its boundaries, is a sheet of clear water called St Margaret's Loch. Outside the park limits the district is all St Margaret's, and the names are of ancient date, though there is no evidence that the good Queen travelled in this direction. In her journeys between Edinburgh and Fife she always crossed the Forth by the Queen's Ferry.

It was David I., Queen Margaret's youngest son, who founded the Abbey of Holy rood, and, doubtless, mother and son were associated together in the minds of the people for sanctity and generosity to their subjects. The old story tells that David, hunting in the forest, which then extended from the hills to the sea, was confronted by a stag with a cross between its antlers. The stag was in some mysterious way the bearer of a divine message, and King David built an abbey on the spot where it appeared, and named it Holy Rood.

CHAPTER 8

Margaret's Mission

St Margaret's name is worthy of a place among the apostles of Scotland for she completed their noble work and repaired the edifice they had built, when plunder, pillage and lawlessness had well-nigh brought it to ruin.

South Britain had become entirely Christian by the end of the fourth century, but the wild Picts and Scots of Caledonia knew nothing then of the sublime teachings of Christ. It was in 397 A.D. that St Ninian, Scotland's first apostle, came from Rome to evangelise the country between the Sol way and the Clyde. A native of Strathclyde and a Christian from his childhood, he had been early filled with the desire of converting his fellow-countrymen, and distrustful of self, as the saints ever are, he had gone to the city of St Peter the better to learn what he so longed to teach to others.

The gospel made good progress under the zealous missionary and he built at Whithorn in Galloway, a church of stone which was known as "*Candida Casa*." It was the first Christian church and also the first stone building in northern Britain.

But just as Christianity began to brighten the country north of the Solway it suffered an almost total eclipse in south Britain. When the barbarian hordes of northern Europe came down on the Roman Empire, it was thought necessary to withdraw the Roman soldiers from Britain, and thus its people were left to the mercy of the Picts and Scots.

Unused for hundreds of years to defend themselves, the Britons felt helpless and unnerved, and called for aid to the wild tribes of Germany—Jutes, Angles and Saxons. The Germans came and did good service, but looking on the fair country for which they were fighting, they became enamoured of its beauty and resolved to make it their own, The Britons, they decided, were unworthy to possess what they were unable to defend. The Picts and Scots utterly routed, and driven back to their strongholds among the Grampians, the Britons feasted their allies and sent them away with rich presents and joyful leave-takings. Alas! Before many months had sped the German tribes appeared again—allies no longer, but enemies. The poor Britons were slaughtered in their homes or driven to the hills, and the Angles and Saxons were masters of the country within a few weeks of their landing.

Soon it was Britain no longer but England, and a pagan England, for the newcomers worshipped Odin and Thor, and Christianity was expelled along with the hapless Britons.

Meanwhile, a Christian boy named Succat was tending the flocks of his father, the Roman citizen, Calpurnius, on the banks of the Clyde in North Britain, when a band of marauders made a raid on his home and carried him into captivity. He was sold as a slave in the north of Ireland, and found himself again tending sheep with the sea between him and his native land. Succat hated his captive state, though he loved the green land of his captivity. Escaping at last, he found his way to France and afterwards to Rome. In both places rich and powerful friends awaited him, brilliant opportunities were given him, and, resolving to study for the priesthood, he became famous alike for zeal and piety. The Pope had sent St Palladius to preach the Gospel to the Irish, but such was not God's design.

When the slave-boy was fleeing from the land of his captivity he had a dream or vision, in which the children of Ireland called on him to teach them the faith of Christ. "Come back to us," they cried. "Bring us the glad tidings." Years had passed since then, but, waking or sleeping, Succat heard the wailing cry of Ireland's children, and now, when the Pope found that Palladius had failed in his mission, and was dead, he sent Succat to convert Ireland. And so, with the apostolic blessing and the name of Patrick, conferred on him by the successor of St Peter, the Apostle of Ireland set out on his great mission of love. He was accompanied by a number of priests and monks eager to assist him in his work.

It was early in the fifth century that St Patrick began his work and never did missionary meet with such success. He had only to speak in order to be obeyed, and in thirty years from his arrival Ireland was a Christian country from north to south and from east to west. St Patrick made thorough conversions, and succeeding generations named the country of his love, the "Island of the Saints."

It was Caledonia that gave St Patrick to Ireland, and before long Ireland returned the favour in generous measure, giving not one but many missionaries to Caledonia. St Columba, the first and greatest, was the son of a king, but he is better known as a saint and an apostle. The disciple of one of St Patrick's most earnest converts, he had all the great missionary's zeal for spreading the gospel and in 563 A.D. he came to Caledonia to win his kindred, the Scots of Dalriada, to the faith of Christ. He founded a monastery on Iona, one of a chain of barren islands off the west coast of Scotland, and gathered many disciples around him, men of learning and goodness whose only desire was to serve God and work for the salvation of souls.

When the time was ripe, St Columba's monks were sent north, south and east to convert the Picts and Scots. Everywhere they met with success, and churches were built that the Sacrifice of the Mass might be celebrated with due honour, from the Orkney and Shetland Islands in the north to Northumbria in the south. Superstition died hard, it is true, and the Picts, especially, often relapsed into the excesses of their pagan days, but slowly and surely the Cross triumphed, and idolatry was vanquished. The Scots were nobler than the Picts and more easily responded to the demands made upon their conduct by the teaching of Christianity.

There were drawbacks, indeed, and it must not be thought that St Columba's work was as easy in the doing, or as thorough when accomplished, as St Patrick's had been. The conversion of Caledonia presented difficulties of various kinds. Its missionaries had to penetrate wild mountain fastnesses and deep glens, to cross lakes and arms of the sea, and to preach to people of many races hardened by idolatrous habits. The monks were not numerous enough to dwell long among their converts to give them all the instruction and training they required, and so it happened that there were frequent relapses into superstition and vice when the teachers of truth and virtue had passed on their way.

Notwithstanding all this, the good work went on with little opposition for nearly two hundred years, and, as Christianity grew in strength, it wrought great changes in northern Britain. In the south, civilisation had brought Christianity, but in the north it was Christianity itself that was the civilising influence. The gospel brought peace and with it desires for order and settlement. Race differences became less marked; hatred and jealousy were overcome for Christ's sake, and gradually the four races which had long struggled for the mastery north of the Solway, became one nation.

Kenneth McAlpine, crowned at Scone in 844 A.D., was the first king of Scots and Picts. He was the more readily accepted by both peoples because his father was a Scot and his mother a Pict, but the Scots were really in the ascendancy, and under Kenneth's rule, the country began to be called Scotland. It was not, however, till his grandson Malcolm II. routed the king of the Lothians at Carham in 1018, that the Tweed became the boundary between England and Scotland. Monasteries soon arose on the mainland as well as on the islands, and education began to be appreciated and sought after. Every monastery had its school, and youths and men were eager to avail themselves of the opportunities thus given them. It was the aim of the monks to train young men and bring them up in piety and learning, that they might carry on the good work in the future, when their elders had been gathered to their reward.

Meanwhile, what of South Britain and its heathen conquerors? Everybody has heard the pretty story of Father Gregory and the English slaves in the Roman market-place. The monk was in the habit of receiving alms from rich people and spending the money in ransoming slaves. One day while going about his charitable work as usual, he saw, exposed for sale among the olive-skinned, dark-haired children of the South, a group of boys and girls of dazzling fairness, with masses of golden hair curling about their shoulders, and eyes as blue as the southern skies in summer.

"Who are these children," cried the monk in wondering admiration.

"They are Angles," answered the keeper.

"Not Angles, but angels," was Father Gregory's quick reply, and straightway he registered a vow that, God willing, he would bring to the nation of these fair children the glad light of the gospel and the sweet teachings of the religion of Christ.

The Romans loved Father Gregory too well to let him go, and soon, as Pope Gregory with all Christendom to rule, he had reluctantly to abandon the idea of ever himself seeing England. He might, however, entrust to others the work of its conversion and he turned his thoughts to the zealous monks in his own dear monastery. Thus it happened that in 597 A.D., the very year that St Columba died at Iona, St Augustine landed on the coast of Kent, sent by Pope Gregory with forty monks to convert England.

The conversion of South Britain is not a tale of victory like that of Ireland. Successes and failures followed each other in bewildering succession, and often after a whole district or kingdom—for there were many kingdoms in England then—had received the true faith, it relapsed into heathenism under a new king or after a fierce war.

Triumph came at last and St Columba's monks, coming southward to Northumbria on missionary labours intent, met and helped the sons of St Augustine in their great work. The Danes and trouble were coming to England in the near future, but the Christianity brought by St Augustine was never lost to its people again until the days of Henry VIII. and the Reformation.

But we must return to Scotland. The sun shone brightly there for a space, and the sky seemed blue and unclouded, but appearances are often deceptive and in the distance a cloud was forming that would soon bring storm and disaster.

The terrible Northmen had appeared several times off the coast of Scotland, and in 800 A.D., they came down like a tempest on the western islands. They hated Christianity and, always cruel, their fury raged most fiercely where they found it. The monasteries of the islands, including that of Iona, were soon but heaps of smouldering ruins, while monks and people were ruthlessly slaughtered. In the years of peace that had preceded this terrible invasion, treasures had begun to accumulate at the various shrines, through the generosity of a devoted people, and now money, sacred vessels, everything of value was carried off by the Northmen. Not only did they come, but they remained and made the islands their own. Heathenism reigned supreme again, and only the blackened remains of church and monastery were left to tell that Christianity had been there.

Sometimes in the course of the next two centuries, the Christians, encouraged by comparative peace, would gather together and build a church, but soon another wild raid would leave the ashes of church and priests and people mingled together. The last fierce slaughter of monks was as late as 986 A.D.

The mainland as well as the islands had to endure the incursions of the Northmen. It is true, they never secured a permanent footing there, but religion suffered woefully from their visits. The monasteries and churches were the chosen objects of attack, for experience on the islands had taught the marauders that the sacred vessels of the altar were the richest booty. Hundreds of devoted monks were slain and with monasteries, schools and teachers swept away, there were few capable of replacing them. The blood of the martyrs is the seed of the Church, but seed grows slowly. Scotland was to reap an abundant harvest in the future, but she had to wait long and suffer much before her day of rejoicing. Rome, the fountain-head of Christianity was far away—we can scarcely realise how far in our days, when trains and steamers and postal and telegraph service, make transit and communication so easy and rapid. The news of Scotland's sufferings and spiritual desolation travelled slowly, but, even if it had not been so, every country of Europe, rising up with difficulty from the ruins of conquest, had need of its own priests and missionaries to convert its conquerors.

Poor Scotland! It was only beginning to find its way in the paths of civilisation and was ill-prepared for such a cruel blow. Children grew up with scarce a teacher to tell them what or why to believe. Education was no longer possible except in a few far-separated parts, and ignorance spread over the land far more rapidly than learning had done. The people were only semi-barbarians after all and the wonder is not that the nation soon became lax and ignorant with regard to religion, but that a remnant of Catholic truth was still kept and cherished in spite of every drawback. And it was thus kept and cherished. When St Margaret came to Scotland in 1069 there were still monks at Dunkeld and St Andrew's and secular priests had succeeded the martyred sons of St Columba in other places.

Ignorance, indeed, had done its work, and though many of the priests were good and devoted men, and as full of zeal as the monks themselves, they were all too few to cope with the great work which had to be done. In such troubled times as followed the destruction of the monasteries the beauty of God's House was thought of not at all. Poor as the monks of St Columba had been in all that concerned themselves, they loved to beautify the altar, and so they had rich chalices and valuable ornaments in their churches. Nothing of value escaped the Northmen, and when they had passed by, new beginnings were necessary everywhere.

The Christians soon built churches of some sort to replace the demolished buildings, but they were rude and poor, with walls of mud and wattle, and roofs of thatch. Pillage of such churches would be an easy matter and so it was not thought advisable to give them rich furnishings. To do so would only encourage the foreign robbers, by providing treasure for them to steal. So thought the fathers; but sons grew up who had no memories of beautiful altars, with rich ornaments and treasures sacrificed and consecrated to the service of God.

They had only seen poor and neglected places of worship, and their minds soared no higher.

And then, alas! As ignorance and indifference spread abroad many entered the churches so seldom as scarcely to know how they were furnished. There was only one bishop in all Scotland, and with means of communication almost non-existent it was impossible for him to keep in touch with his scattered flock. Abuses crept in, the laws of the Church were disregarded, and men and women forgot the high ideals that the disciples of St Columba had placed before them. The light of Christianity was slowly but surely waning when God sent St Margaret to stir up its dying embers and make them glow again.

St Margaret did not substitute for an ancient Celtic Christianity that of Rome as some writers of history pretend.

"There was indeed no need for Margaret to bring a new religion into Scotland" says Mr Freeman "but she gave a new life to the religion which she found existing there." Margaret had been a Catholic in Hungary, and in England, and when she came to Scotland she found there only her own dear faith, living still in spite of ignorance and consequent neglect and decay.

The good Queen understood these things better than later reformers because she was humble. She never thought of trying to improve on the teaching of Christ and His apostles or of inventing a new religion for her poor erring people. All she sought to do—and she did it nobly—was to build up what had been broken down, to correct mistakes and eradicate abuses that had found entrance through national prejudice and isolation. Though the Church seemed to be falling into decay, its foundations were strong and secure. St Margaret's design was to clear away the debris of ruin, and to set enthusiastic builders to work, that the structure might be restored to its former beauty.

St Ninian and St Columba had taught the people to believe in Christ and this they had not forgotten. St Margaret came to remind them that "faith without works is dead," and that Our Lord would have them not only know His life but live it. As St John tells us "*He that saith he knoweth Him and keepeth not His commandments is a liar and the truth is not in him.*"

The Queen's own faith was strong and living, and because she knew her Lord she loved and served Him. It was her aim and the work of her life, thus to vivify religion in her court and throughout Scotland and to make it not only known but also lived and loved,

CHAPTER 9

Margaret and the Churches

I have loved, O Lord, the beauty of thy house and the place where thy glory dwelleth.

St Margaret was no strong-minded young woman, setting out for Scotland on a mission of conversion. A humble retiring maiden, princess though she was, brought up in seclusion from the world and dreaming of a still more secluded life in the cloister, she would have appeared to human wisdom all unsuited for such a mighty task.

But God uses the weak things of the world to confound the strong, and as His hand guided her frail boat in the stormy waters of the Forth, so it guided her gentle spirit in the work for His glory which He had sent her to accomplish in Scotland.

The Saxon Princess found herself among rude surroundings in Dunfermline, as we have seen, but probably the bareness and uncared-for appearance of the chapel was her greatest trial; for she was ever mindful of God's honour, and had always seen his altars adorned with the best that His people could offer Him, of what He, Himself, had given them. As soon as she became Queen of Scotland, and mistress of the Tower, she set to work to make the chapel a more worthy dwelling-place for our Lord. Her most beautiful ornaments were sacrificed for its adornment and the first vestments made by her ladies were for the priests who said Mass at its altar. All this was not enough. It grieved St Margaret's loving heart that there was no church in Scotland large and beautiful like those of the South, and her devoted husband rejoiced because she had a desire that he could satisfy.

Thus it came to pass that a new church rose up on the heights behind Dunfermline Tower, a stately building which had at its completion the renown of being the "largest and fairest" in all the land. This,

75

however, was not remarkable praise, for Scottish churches were few and small until long after this date. It was left to St Margaret's sons to cover Scotland with fine buildings for the greater honour of God.

The Dunfermline church was completed in 1074 and dedicated to the Holy Trinity. As there are three Persons in One God, the chroniclers tell us, the King and Queen offered their church to God with a threefold intention—to thank Him for their happy meeting and union at Dunfermline; to beg His grace, that they might accomplish the salvation of their souls; and to ask His blessing on their children in this world and in the next. St Margaret delighted in adorning the new church, despoiling herself of her most precious jewels that it might be beautified. Turgot says there were in this church "many vessels of pure and solid gold for the sacred service of the altar, and about which I can speak with the greater certainty since by the Queen's orders, I myself for a long time had all of them under my charge." Here indeed the Queen placed her greatest treasure, a crucifix of "priceless value," covered with gold and studded with gems.

This church of the Holy Trinity built by St Margaret was the first of several noble buildings consecrated to the service of God which were erected on this site by her successors. It was also the ancestor of the present degenerate edifice whose tower with its huge letters, proclaiming the honour of "King Robert the Bruce," proclaims at the same time its modern construction. A monastery soon grew up beside the good Queen's church and in the latter and its successors, built by St Margaret's children, the office of the Church was chanted by the monks of Dunfermline, until they were silenced and scattered in 1593 by the "Lords of the Congregation," who enriched themselves with the patrimony of the poor, in the name of reformation.

There is no pitiful tale of relaxation and decay in the history of Dunfermline Abbey. It had a long line of distinguished abbots, who indeed acquired much wealth and attained to great power, but who used both for the glory of God and the good of their fellow-men.

Dunfermline and the surrounding districts owe their prosperity to their ancient Abbey, for "it is good to dwell under the crozier" as their ancestors did. The forests were cleared by the devoted labours of the monks, the land was laboriously put under cultivation and happy homesteads sheltered the prosperous descendants of the poor men and women for whom St Margaret's charity had done so much in days when there was no work to be had. All the Queen's good works were ably perpetuated by the monks. They had schools for the studi-

DUNFERMLINE ABBEY.

ous and workshops where those so inclined might learn the various crafts. They taught men how to till the soil and make it fruitful, how to build houses, how to trade with other countries, how, in a word, to become industrious and ingenious and resourceful, like the people of more civilised countries.

But, better than all this, the monks were the guardians of the unfortunate. They nursed the sick, took care of the simple, fed and clothed the poor, and provided employment for all who could work. There was no need for any on the Abbey lands to be idle, uncared for, or erring, for the monks were interested in all the wants of their people, whether of soul or body. While St Margaret was making herself acquainted with the state of religion in Scotland she had occasion to study in considerable detail the life and work of St Columba, and her admiration for the apostolic man grew with her greater knowledge of him.

Earl Thorfinn, the Norwegian ruler of the Hebrides, whose widow, Ingibiorg, became Malcolm Canmore's first wife, died in 1057, and from that time the Western Isles were governed by an Irish prince. In 1072 they fell into the hands of Canmore and remained under his government until the last year of his reign, when he ceded them again to Magnus, King of Norway.

No sooner were the Western Isles in St Margaret's power than she bethought herself of Iona and resolved to restore its ancient glory to the best of her ability. She rebuilt the monastery and church, brought monks from other houses and settled them there, providing a suitable endowment for their support. Ruin came again when the Norwegians re-established themselves on the islands, and succeeding restorations were followed again by ruin, and yet, if St Columba 's prophecy is to be fulfilled, the monks will once more chant the divine office on the wild island of the Atlantic.

Isle of my heart, isle of my love,
Instead of the voice of the monks
Shall be the lowing of kine;
But ere the world come to an end,
Iona shall be as it was.

Many churches throughout Scotland benefited by St Margaret's generosity. Her rooms in the palace were perfect workshops of sacred art, with copes, chasubles, stoles and priestly vestments of every kind, in all stages of preparation. Her maids of honour became experts in embroidery and their mistress sent their beautiful work over all the land. Nor was this all. The Queen established,, other kinds of workshops outside the palace, and brought skilled craftsmen from England and the Continent to teach her own subjects how to fashion golden vases and candle- sticks and other beautiful things for the poor neglected churches.

Meanwhile, the services of the Church were celebrated at Dunfermline with splendour and solemnity, for the Saxon monks helped the Queen in all her good works with glad and grateful hearts. They had long looked with apprehension on the general stagnation but their feeble efforts had been powerless to stay its course, and now it seemed that God had heard their prayers and given them their hearts' desire. Men came to Mass in the new Abbey Church and pondered on the significance of what they saw there. It was surely more in accordance with the teachings of their faith than anything they had known hitherto. Religion had been but a secondary consideration, not to be taken seriously except by priests, and monks and nuns shut up in their cloister away from the world. Yet here was a queen, young, beautiful and learned, and she was very evidently persuaded that religion was the "one thing necessary," for she made so many sacrifices for its sake that none could doubt her sincerity. Her goods, her talents, her time, were given ungrudgingly that God's House might be made more worthy of His Presence and there she might be seen kneeling in humble abasement before the altar, adoring her Lord like the lowliest of her people.

It did not come at once, but ere many years had passed, we hear of the nobles and their ladies following the example set by the Queen, and, like her, despoiling themselves to make the churches beautiful. Crowded congregations became the rule as time went on, and larger buildings had to be raised to accommodate them. Ladies took pleasure in working for the altars, and learned with eagerness the arts which the good Queen's needlewomen were as eager to teach, and many of them found new interest in life as they bent over fine linen and laces, and cloth of gold and silver, fashioning these dainty materials into altar-cloths and vestments.

External reforms! Yes. St Margaret knew that as well as we moderns do, but love grows in strength and power of sacrifice, when we labour and deny ourselves for those we love, and St Margaret knew this, too. The outward attention to religion went hand in hand with a great renewal of fervour and an improvement in manners and morals, and so the dead bones of Scottish Christianity began to live again. And as St Margaret raised up and made beautiful the material churches, in order that Christ might be duly honoured, so she was going to raise up again and clothe with honour His Mystic Church, which, in this land of her adoption, had fallen into well-nigh as great decay and ruin.

CHAPTER 10

Margaret, Apostle of Scotland

It was comparatively an easy matter for St Margaret to convert the King and remodel the court. Her example and influence were so powerful that she early won her husband, as an ancient writer somewhat strongly expresses it, "to relinquish his barbarous manners, and live honestly and civilly." Turgot marvels how "by the help of God, she made him most attentive to the works of justice, mercy, almsgiving and other virtues," as well as to prayer. Her household and following were likewise soon composed of practical Christians, who, like the Queen herself, found joy and delight in serving God.

But St Margaret could not be content with the conversion of her household only. There was all the rest of Scotland to be thought of, and the land was now her land, and the people her people. She could not be happy in the light while they were in darkness. The Queen's investigations had brought to her notice many things that needed reform, for, partly through ignorance, partly through neglect, some strange practices existed in different parts of the country—practices contrary to the usage of the universal Church. Turgot tells us some of these practices, though he is not as explicit as we could desire. At a much earlier date than this the sons of St Columba and those of St Augustine had been at variance concerning some matters of Church discipline, and notably the date of Easter. The dispute had been happily settled long ago, and for two centuries and more Scotland had kept Easter with the rest of the world.

And now in the eleventh century St Margaret found them in error as to the other end of Lent, for these tantalising people had a date entirely their own for its commencement. While all other Catholics throughout Christendom began the fast on the Wednesday preceding the first Sunday of Lent, the Scots alone began on the Monday of the first week. Moreover, with a hardness and rigour quite opposed to the sweet mercy of the Gospel teaching, and the traditions of the Church, the Scots refused to receive the Holy Eucharist even at Easter, alleging that they were not worthy, though they had been absolved from their sins in the tribunal of Penance. Some of the priests defended this attitude and often forbade those who had sinned grievously to approach the Altar at any time, even when penitent and purified by a good confession.

The mere telling of it shocks us, and yet our ancestors only made the same mistake as many well-meaning people make in the twentieth century, that of looking on the Holy Eucharist as a reward for virtue, rather than as a means of attaining to it. "*He that eateth Me, the same also shall live by Me*," says our Lord; but, in spite of this, some refuse to go to Holy Communion daily, or even weekly, because they are not "good enough," forgetting that by depriving themselves of the "*Bread which cometh down from Heaven*," they are starving their souls and hindering themselves in the very attainment of "goodness."

In some parts of Scotland there was another peculiar abuse. Mass was celebrated by a strange and barbarous rite. Turgot does not explain this rite further than by saying that it was "contrary to the usage of the whole Church," and there are many conjectures as to its nature. Some think that ancient superstitious practices were mingled with the ceremonial and others that Gaelic was used instead of Latin, but history is silent on the matter and the actual truth will probably never be known. A fourth blot on the Catholic life of Scotland was the disregard shown for Sunday. Many ignored the obligation of hearing Mass and business was conducted as on other days. Finally the laws of the Church with regard to marriage were violated in a shocking manner and especially those relating to kinship.

When these and other abuses were reported to the good Queen, she spent many hours before the Altar praying for light and guidance in her difficult task. It was evident that the people of Scotland were gradually falling back into the ways of life from which St Columba and his disciples had rescued them, and she could not be indifferent to their fate. She had already done much by her good example; and priests, like her confessor, Turgot, had helped her to reach many who were beyond her personal influence, but all this was not enough. St Margaret's conscience said to her, as Mardochai had said to Esther of old:—

And who knoweth whether thou art not therefore come to the kingdom
that thou mightest be ready in such a time as this?

The Celtic priests ignored the Queen's messengers because they
did not mean to be convinced of the error of their ways, and then,
after more consideration and prayer, St Margaret took a step which
was surely a brave one for a gentle lady who loved so well the seclusion and retirement of her own home. Her plan was to try the effect
of personal expostulation with her chief opponents, and the King not
only approved but eagerly undertook to help her. The most important
among the clergy were invited to a conference on the disputed points,
but the Queen could not speak Gaelic, and though the priests used
Latin in the Church services there were few whose knowledge of it
was sufficient for argument.

The King simplified matters by acting as interpreter, being equally
at home in the use of Gaelic and Saxon, and he seems to have acted
throughout only as St Margaret's mouthpiece. It was an eloquent tes-
timony to Malcolm's love and reverence for his wife, for he was a man
who liked being in the foreground and was little used to second places
either in the council-chamber or on the battlefield. There were many
conferences or councils, but Turgot tells us chiefly of one which lasted
for three days. The Culdees defended their position on every point,
but the Queen's reasoning was logical and conclusive and point by
point they yielded and agreed to do as she desired.

These men (*Keledei* or *Ceile De*, servants of God) were priests living in community. They were the successors of the monks of St Columba, destroyed by the Danes, but did not live according to the strict
rule of their predecessors. As to Lent, they maintained that they fasted
for six weeks on the authority of the Gospel which tells that Christ
fasted for such a period. St Margaret reminded them that the Gospel
expressly says "forty days."

"As to fasting for forty days," she continued, "it is a thing which
notoriously you do not do. For seeing that during the six weeks, you
deduct the six Sundays from the fast, it is clear that thirty-six days only
remain."

When asked why they did not obey the laws of the Church with
regard to the Easter Communion, the priests quoted St Paul—

He that eateth and drinketh unworthily, eateth and drinketh judgment
to himself.

"As we are sinners," they said, "we fear to approach the Sacred

Mystery, lest we merit this condemnation."

"But we are all sinners," said the Queen, "even the infant who has lived but a day, and if none of us, being sinners, ought to receive, why did our Lord Himself say:—'*Unless you eat the Flesh of the Son of Man and drink His Blood, you shall not have life in you.*'"

Continuing her discourse, St Margaret reminded the Culdees that their quotation from St Paul was incomplete as they had omitted the words:—"*Not discerning the Body of the Lord,*" that is, not making a distinction between the Blessed Sacrament, which is the Body of the Lord, and ordinary bread. It was the man, she told them, who would dare to approach in mortal sin without confession or penance, who would "*eat and drink judgment to himself.*" "Whereas we," she said, "who many days previously have made confession of our sins and have been cleansed from their stains by chastening penance, by trying fasts, by almsgiving and tears—approaching in the Catholic faith to the Lord's Table on the Day of His Resurrection, receive the Body and Blood of Jesus Christ, the immaculate Lamb, not to judgment, but to the remission of our sins, and as a health-giving preparation for eternal happiness."

When St Margaret had won the priests to her side on such important matters, and in doing so gained their esteem and reverence, it was easy to induce them to use their authority for the abolition of the "barbarous rite" used in saying Mass. Turgot assures us that it disappeared at once, "so that henceforth," he says, "in the whole of Scotland, there was not one single person who dared to continue the practice." Still more easily the Queen won her adversaries to help her in making the people observe the sanctity of Sunday. They had no argument in favour of non-observance, for the evil customs had established themselves gradually owing to neglect and carelessness. St Margaret herself was always most careful that all under her care should keep the Sunday holy, and many distinguished Protestants consider that the strictly kept Scottish "Sabbath" is a product of her zeal. The reverence may indeed have come down from St Margaret though the manner of showing it is different.

At the close of the conference the priests were in perfect accord with the Queen on each point discussed, and promised to use every effort to make their flocks all that she desired them to be. They left St Margaret's presence marvelling at her power and also at their own docility. They would have defied alike the eloquence of the Saxon monks and the might of Canmore's sword, but they had bowed down their stubborn wills before the sweet influence of a good and gentle woman.

Other conferences were held, but they were rather to arrange ways and means than to settle differences. St Margaret had no idea of taking on herself any part of Church government. The priests were the proper teachers of the people, and she neither did their work nor sent anyone else to do it. Her care was to make them love Rome and all its ways, for she knew well that the branch can only have the fullness of life when entirely united to the vine.

Perfect harmony as to religious ceremonial and observance was soon established between the Scottish Church and the rest of the Christian world, and it was never broken again until the sixteenth century. Gradually the apparently dying Church came back to strong and vigorous life. St Columba had sowed the seed, St Margaret watered and tended the rising grain, and God gave the increase.

CHAPTER 11

Margaret's Journeys

In the early days of Scotland's existence as a kingdom, the monarch was in the habit of making royal progresses throughout his dominions that he might know his subjects better, and make and administer suitable laws for the furtherance of civilisation. Duncan is represented as travelling about in this way and being with his attendants the guest of one of his own Thanes. Shakespeare, in fact, makes a visit of this kind to the castle of Macbeth the occasion of Duncan's murder by his treacherous host.

Malcolm, the son of Duncan, made such progresses also, though probably, with his two royal abodes of Edinburgh and Dunfermline, he made fewer state visits than his predecessors.

Later kings managed still better. They had estates in every part of the country, and spent with their courts part of the year at each in turn. Thus royalty became better known and a greater number of people were able to profit by the court expenditure.

It is believed that St Margaret accompanied her husband on his progresses, and a story has come down to us which certainly suggests a journey through wilder country than lay between Dunfermline and Lothian.

When Edgar Atheling came to Scotland in 1069, there was in his train a young noble named Bartulph, who enjoyed the fullest confidence of the Prince and his mother. Malcolm Canmore soon came to appreciate his worth also, and when Princess Margaret became his Queen, Bartulph was appointed her chamberlain.

Among the duties of the Queen's chamberlain there was one which seems peculiar in our days of easy and comfortable travelling. When Queen Margaret went abroad in difficult country—and there was little else in Scotland in the eleventh century—she rode behind

Bartulph on his horse, and his was the responsibility of bringing her safely through river and morass. On one occasion a royal progress had been postponed several times on account of heavy rains but at last a bright morning allowed the party to set out. The chamberlain choosing his ground carefully for the Queen's greater convenience, was somewhat in the rear, and when he reached a certain river, he found that King Malcolm and his attendants had made a detour and crossed higher up. This indeed was the ordinary ford, but the river was in spate and the black waters rushed past with threatening force. Bartulph hesitated, when he thought of the Queen behind him, and proposed following the King, but St Margaret laughed at his fears and urged instant crossing that she might rejoin her husband.

The Queen's safety demanded some extra precaution, however, and the chamberlain insisted that his royal mistress should put round her waist a stout leathern belt which he fastened by means of a large buckle to his own trappings. Secured in this way it was impossible for the Queen to fall while the chamberlain maintained his seat. They entered the water and proceeded without much difficulty until they reached midstream where the rush of the torrent was wildest. Here the horse floundered helplessly, and but for Bartulph's forethought, the Queen would certainly have been swept away by the angry waters. She slipped several times and with some difficulty regained her seat, but she maintained her self-possession and said no word to her chamberlain, whose entire attention was given to his struggling horse. At last the poor animal found foothold and began to make some progress and then Bartulph had time to glance at the Queen. "Grip hard," he cried, raising his voice that it might be heard above the noise of the waters; "we'll win owre yet."

Queen Margaret was clinging with desperation to the leathern belt. She was wet and cold, but she had not lost her sense of humour. "Gin the buckle bide," she answered grimly, her eyes fixed on her only hope of safety, which was strained to its utmost tension.

The buckle did "bide," and soon the Queen's ladies removed from their royal mistress all traces of her misadventure. When a radiant Queen, clad again in beautiful garments, laughingly gave a graphic description of the struggle in the river, Bartulph was warmly complimented by the King. At Queen Margaret's request the chamberlain received the royal command to adorn his shield with buckles and to take for the motto of his family the words "*Grip hard*." Bartulph had already obtained from the King a grant of lands in Fife. Somewhat later he married the King's sister, and either he or his son Malcolm acquired an estate of considerable size and value in Aberdeenshire. From these lands the family took the name of Leslie, and became an important Scottish house. The Leslie shield still has its band of buckles and the ancient motto reminds the descendants of Bartulph to "Grip hard."

In connection with St Margaret's travels we learn a secret which makes us cease to wonder at God's merciful dealings with Scotland. Always ready to forgive many sinners for the sake of a few just men, He found more than a few in poor Scotland in spite of its decadence. All over the country, in mountain fastnesses, in the depth of the forest, by the wild seashore, and on the lonely islands of mountain lakes there were holy men, living in caves or in cells of their own construction. They were called anchorites, and the people held them in great esteem on account of the strictness of their lives. Turgot says that they lived "in the flesh, but not according to the flesh; for being upon earth, they led the life of angels."

In most cases the anchorites lived entirely alone, far from human habitations, but sometimes several had cells in the same neighbourhood, that they might profit by the ministrations of a priest among their number. Their lives were passed in silence and prayer and manual labour after the manner of the "Fathers of the Desert," but they were always ready with help and counsel when people came to them in distress or difficulty. Many of the holy men were Scots, but some were Saxons driven into exile by Norman tyranny. Passing years indeed brought peace to England, and the wanderers might have returned home, but, enamoured of their solitary life, they preferred the place of their exile.

St Margaret loved to visit these hermits, conversing with them on spiritual subjects and recommending herself to their prayers, "for in them she loved and venerated Christ." She would fain have made them presents, but they refused to accept anything, and so she begged them to set her tasks from time to time in works of mercy and almsgiving. This they did readily enough, and the good Queen delighted in obeying their directions minutely. In this way many poor people received assistance, and miseries of every kind were alleviated. One good work often suggested another, and St Margaret gave time, trouble, and money ungrudgingly in her neighbours' service. Nor had she any difficulty in finding poor people to help. News of her comings and goings travelled quickly, and wherever she halted crowds of unfortunates surrounded her. Widows and orphans were always numerous in these gatherings. They flocked to the kind Queen "as they would have done to a loving mother, and none of them left her without being comforted."

St Margaret always took care on leaving home to provide herself with abundant alms, and often when she had emptied her purse she would give away all that she could spare of her wearing apparel. Her attendants were ready to help by handing over to the Queen all that they could dispense with for the time being, in order that none of the poor might go away empty-handed. Turgot says that both ladies and gentlemen in the Queen's following were always glad to be despoiled in this manner and strove who should offer most, for, as he quaintly remarks, they knew from experience that their kind mistress "would pay them back two-fold." This is the only fault that even modern writers can find in St Margaret. Some of them think that her indiscriminate almsgiving was unwise and tended to encourage mendicancy. It is a wide question in our own day, this of indiscriminate almsgiving, and probably as many err on the wrong side as on the right, but if we transport ourselves back to the eleventh century among St Margaret's poor, we shall find circumstances even more perplexing than they are now.

In the wild Scotland of primitive times there was no self-made poverty to fight with, for the vices that now keep so many squalidly poor have come in the wake of civilisation. The poor of the eleventh century were for the most part, those whom war and lawlessness had deprived of their breadwinners and the captives whose hard lot of slavery kept them always destitute. St Margaret might have sent her attendants to disperse the crowds, and the poor creatures could have crept back to their miserable huts to starve and die, but that was not the kind of lesson the good Queen gave. Why could they not work? Some were old and feeble and some were weak and ill. There are institutions for such wretched ones in the twentieth century, but there were none in the eleventh.

And even for the able-bodied what means of earning a livelihood was there in primitive times? The slaves had to toil without remuneration and in the establishments of the time their service was sufficient. So far there were no industries and little agriculture. In times of war the men could fight and in times of peace they could hunt and fish, but when death or disease struck down the head of a poor family, there was nothing but starvation for the hapless wife and children.

St Margaret did not repulse her beggars to teach them not to beg.

She helped as many as she could and taught those around her sweet lessons of charity that sank deep into their hearts and brought forth abundant fruit, not only in their own lives but in those of their children and their children's children. It was not that she considered this mere supplying of present needs a good plan. We see her at the same time thinking of the ages to come, and laying the foundations of a system that would make alms-giving of the kind she practised unnecessary on the part of her successors. Her kind heart realised, however, that it would be sorry consolation to the hungry around her to tell them that their grandchildren would have plenty, and so she fed them, while maturing plans for the future.

Meanwhile Queen Margaret encouraged the establishment of foreign industries in Scotland, and founded monasteries that the poor might have permanent guardians. Her sons followed in their mother's footsteps and so in the course of years, the seed planted by the good Queen grew into a large and beneficent tree. "It is good to live under the crozier" and during the period when the monasteries were fervent and flourishing, poverty was practically unknown. As we have seen in the case of Dunfermline Abbey, the monks provided employment in school, workshop or field for all who were able to work, and they sheltered and cared for the old and infirm without remuneration of any kind. There was a secret in their charity, too, which we seem to have lost in the intervening centuries, for they could relieve a man's needs without stealing his self-respect.

St Andrew's had been the ecclesiastical centre of Scotland for many years before the coming of St Margaret. According to an ancient legend the Apostle's relics had been brought to Fife in a manner which had something of the miraculous about it. St Regulus or St Rule had a dream or vision in which he was told by an angel to carry the bones of St Andrew from Patras to Scotland. The saintly messenger braved every danger and had almost performed his task, but storms are frequent on the coasts of Fife and his boat encountered a fierce one. Poor St Regulus was ship-wrecked at Muckros, and barely succeeded in saving his own life and bringing ashore the precious relics. A church was built where he landed and Muckros became St Andrew's. The story is told of the fourth century, but historians can find no mention of the relics earlier than the eighth century, when they certainly reposed under the altar of St Andrew's Church. St Andrew's had long been the seat of the "High-Bishop" of Scotland, and in St Margaret's time he began to be called "Bishop of St Andrew's."

Devout people in Scotland had for centuries been in the habit of making pilgrimages to the shrine of St Andrew, but with the new religious life that St Margaret had awakened in the country, stirring men's hearts to their depths, the pilgrims became very numerous. Acting on the suggestion of her anchorites, probably those of Loch Leven, whom she is said to have regarded with much reverence, the Queen set herself to provide for the comfort of these pilgrims. Many of them had to cross the Forth, and the Queen had houses built on both shores that they might have suitable shelter. The sites of Queen Margaret's hostels are covered now by the villages of North and South Queensferry.

Servants were appointed to wait on the pilgrims and provide them with all they needed for rest and refreshment, and no pilgrim might be asked for payment. "Ships" carried the pilgrims across the estuary also free of charge, for the good Queen bore the expense of the whole undertaking herself. Though St Margaret probably never realised it, this first passenger service across the Forth was a considerable step forward in civilisation and progress. Was there any Celtic seer in the pilgrims' boat who could pierce with magic vision the mists of the future, and so looking upward could trace far above him the giant girders of the Forth Bridge? The trains that cross the wonderful structure bear many visitors to St Andrew's, but they are not pilgrims to the shrine of the Apostle. His relics are gone from Fife, and the beautiful cathedral under whose altar they reposed is now only a picturesque ruin.

CHAPTER 12

Margaret—
A Pearl Among Women

"It came to pass," says Turgot, "that this venerable Queen who by God's help had been so desirous to cleanse His House from all stain and error, was found day by day worthier of becoming His temple, as the Holy Spirit shone ever brighter in her heart."

In all her care for others, St Margaret never forgot the needs of her own soul. Secular work instead of distracting her, seemed to draw her closer to God, because in her humility she knew herself to be incapable of doing anything without His help, and she sought it unceasingly by prayer and penance and deeds of mercy. Her victories in conference with the Culdees, and the wonderful success attending all her undertakings, had no power to puff her up or make her attempt things that were beyond her sphere. In her own estimation she was but a faulty and ignorant woman whom God had honoured by using her as His instrument, and to Him she gave the glory when things went well. She was ever ready to consult others and to govern herself by their counsels.

Even in her conferences she would turn to those about her and question them regarding their opinion of the prudence and circumspection of what she was saying and doing. She expected straightforward, truthful answers, too, and was impatient of anything that savoured of flattery. Yet no man in her kingdom possessed a deeper or clearer intellect than hers, and none could express ideas more accurately or aptly. It often happened that the clever men whom she consulted went from her presence wiser than when they entered it, while she remained all unconscious of the impression she had made and only esteemed herself fortunate in having such able advisers. In

England, as Princess Margaret, she had made the acquaintance of Lanfranc, the saintly and learned Norman monk who had then just been appointed Archbishop of Canterbury.

The distinguished prelate wrote to her frequently, after she became Queen of Scotland, and at her earnest petition acted though at a distance as her spiritual father. He advised her also on affairs concerning the Church and her people, and on one occasion, probably that of her first conference with the Culdees, he sent at her request three of his brethren in religion. These made some stay in Scotland, and besides sup- porting the Queen in her conferences, they were of considerable assistance to her in carrying out her reforms.

St Margaret was twenty-four years old when she came to Scotland and for twenty-four years more she was its Queen. "She put out her hand to strong things," and as the years went on, her energies never flagged, nor did she ever grow weary of well-doing. Gradually the court lost all signs of barbarity and assumed the aspect of other Christian courts, and to the Queen as teacher and model was due the credit of the mighty change.

"But," says Turgot, "even as she walked in state, robed in royal splendour, she, like another Esther, in her heart trod all these trappings under foot and bade herself remember that beneath the gold and gems lay only dust and ashes." She had no regard for worldly grandeur in itself, but prudence told her that royal dignity was a means which could be used for great and glorious ends, for the glory of God and the salvation of souls, and so she remodelled the Scottish court. "It was easy," says her confessor, "for her to repress all vain glory arising from earthly splendour since her soul never forgot how transitory is this frail life." In spite of her life of heroic virtue—a life that made the people of Scotland regard her as a saint while she was yet alive—she had the habit of meditating frequently, "tremblingly and fearfully," on the Day of Judgment.

"With this thought," says the holy man, "she often entreated me to rebuke her without hesitation, in private, whenever I saw anything worthy of blame either in her words or actions." Evidently he did not find fault often enough to please his penitent, for she urges him again and again not to be remiss in this duty. "Better," she tells him, "are the wounds of a friend, than the deceitful kisses of an enemy."

St Margaret's favourite study was Holy Scripture, and in the midst of councils, lawsuits, and the distracting cares of state, she always found time to devote to it. Books were few and precious in Scotland in the eleventh century, and Turgot tells us that he exerted himself to obtain copies of the Gospels for the holy Queen, so desirous was she of leading others to love them as dearly as she did herself. At that early date the entire Bible was seldom bound into one volume, and the Gospels were, of course, more frequently transcribed than the books of the Old Testament. Latin, the language of the Church, was understood by the greater number of educated people, and they read the Bible in that language. In the middle ages, however, as the monastery schools multiplied, and learning became more general, there were numerous translations of the Scriptures into the vulgar tongue. Elfric tells us himself that he rendered the Gospels into the language of the country, "for the edification of the simple, who know only that language."

The Gospels were St Margaret's special delight, and she never went anywhere without them. Clever and learned as she was, however, hers was no hard, dry, critical study, but rather what we call meditation. She pondered the sacred words in her heart, prayerfully seeking in them God's message to her own soul, and so by studying the life of Christ, she learnt more and more to walk in the footsteps and imitate the virtues of the God-man.

Turgot tells us a pretty story of St Margaret's favourite book of the Gospels. It is indeed the only incident of a miraculous nature that he permits himself to speak of in connection with the Queen, so strong is his determination to be moderate in his praise and to fail rather by defect than by excess. It is as follows:—

St Margaret had a beautiful book of the Gospels adorned with gold and precious stones and containing richly gilt paintings of the four Evangelists, and capital letters "radiant with gold." No doubt the King was responsible for the gorgeous binding of the book, and the Queen loved it better than any other that she possessed, and always desired to have it brought when she travelled abroad. One day an attendant, carrying the precious volume somewhat carelessly in a loose wrapper, stumbled in crossing a ford, and in regaining a firm footing dropped the book in the water and passed on, unconscious of his loss. Presently the Queen asked for her book, and when it could not be found a diligent search was made for it. A week passed and then a man in the Queen's following had occasion again to cross the ford. What was his surprise and delight to see through the clear water, resting on the pebbles at the bottom of the river, the Queen's book. It was open and its leaves were kept in constant gentle motion by the action of the running water.

The wonderful book was taken from the stream as perfect as if water had never touched it. The current had washed away the silk coverings that had formerly protected the "radiant" letters, but the letters themselves and the leaves of the book were absolutely uninjured. The pages were white, the gold untarnished, the letters undimmed in brightness. Nothing indeed about the volume suggested its watery resting-place except a slender streak like a hair, in the margin of some of the leaves near the edge. The recovered treasure was triumphantly carried to the Queen, and all who saw it, expressed wonder and admiration. St Margaret devoutly gave thanks to God, and valued her book more highly than before. Happily, this relic of the past has not been lost. It is now a priceless treasure in the Bodleian Library, Oxford. In spite of his caution Turgot cannot refrain from attesting his belief that the book was miraculously preserved.

"Whatever others may think," he says, in speaking of St Margaret's holiness, "I for my part believe that this wonder was worked by Our Lord, out of His love for this venerable Queen."

In the "Ages of Faith" it was one of the dearest wishes of a Christian heart to visit the City of St Peter and pray at the shrine of the Apostle. St Margaret's love of Rome was not slow in communicating itself to her people, and so it happened that before she had been many years on the throne, Scotland, like its neighbours, had its little band of pilgrims to the Eternal City. It was a joy to St Margaret to see them go, but her motherly heart yearned over them in their wanderings, and she could not bear to think of them as alone and friendless in the mighty city so far away. Her great mind thought of every- thing, and so it came to pass that Malcolm Canmore at his Queen's request endowed a hospice in Rome for Scottish pilgrims.

Many a Scot making a visit of devotion to the City of the Popes, blessed St Margaret for the kindness and hospitable entertainment he received owing to her loving forethought. And so, going on her way "towards the Heavenly Country, in thought and word and deed," and drawing others to join her as she went "that they might with her attain true happiness," she saw her children growing up around her in beauty and goodness, her husband attaining to such power as no previous king of Scotland had enjoyed, and the country of her adoption learning her lessons so well as to give promise of soon taking an honourable place among Christian nations.

She was the "valiant woman" whose price is "as of things from afar and from the uttermost coasts." It might well be said of her that "her children rose up and called her blessed, her husband, and he praised her," and also that her works would "praise her in the gates." It was an ancient custom to name people from some striking quality or characteristic, and St Margaret might have been so named for she was a "pearl" amongst women.

"She was called Margaret," says Turgot, "and in the sight of God, she showed herself to be a pearl, precious in faith and works."

CHAPTER 13

Margaret and the Cross

A king, the best who possessed Alban.
He was a king, of kings fortunate;
He was the vigilant crusher of enemies;
And there shall not be born for ever
One who had more fortune or greatness.

This is how an ancient writer describes Malcolm Canmore, the husband of St Margaret. It is not a prophetic utterance, but it expresses well the estimation in which the great head was held by his own people.

Scottish history grows distinct and readable with Malcolm's coming. His royal ancestry, indeed, goes back for ages, but his predecessors are shadowy figures, with history and legend so much intermingled around them that it is impossible to separate fact and fable.

Long before the Christian era, says legend, there lived on the banks of the Nile a daughter of the Pharaohs whose name was Scota. She was wise and beautiful far beyond the ordinary daughters of men, but this did not prevent her from being the victim of cruel tyranny on the part of a wicked enemy. To escape his malice Scota resolved to leave her native Egypt forever. With her husband and a band of faithful followers, she launched out into the Mediterranean and sailed away to the west. Scota was rich, for she carried with her in her fleet of boats many precious and beautiful things—gold and silver and precious stones.

Her greatest treasure, however, was none of these valuables, but a huge stone of no beauty whatever. It had long been the heirloom in Scota's family, and her people called it the *Lia Fail* or Stone of Destiny. Tradition said that it was the veritable stone which had formed a pillow for Jacob's head when he saw his wonderful vision. Scota prized the *Lia Fail* above all her possessions, and no wonder. Had not the wise men of her native land foretold that where the *Lia Fail* remained, there Scota's children and her children's children for untold generations should reign as kings?

God gave the exiles clement skies and favourable winds and guided their boats through broad and narrow seas until, one sunny day, the entire party landed on the west coast of Erin. Scota and her people—her husband has left us only his name—settled down in the Green Isle of the West, and were henceforward known as Scots, or the followers of Scota.

In the third and fourth centuries of the Christian era, bands of their descendants seeking a new home, crossed the North Channel and took possession of Dalriada or Argyle. Among these adventurers was a lineal descendant of Scota, though it is not clear how many generations separated him from his great ancestress. This prince brought with him from Erin the great *Lia Fail*, and his descendants the kings of Dalriada preserved it with reverent care.

When in 844 A.D. Kenneth McAlpine became King of both Scots and Picts—the two chief races in Caledonia—he was crowned at Scone on the Stone of Destiny. So, too, all his descendants were crowned, including Malcolm Canmore, until Edward I. carried the Scottish treasure to England after his temporary conquest of Scotland. The "Hammer of the Scots" thought to falsify the ancient prophecy and placed the *Lia Fail* in the English Coronation Chair in Westminster Abbey, where it still remains. And yet, if the old tradition is true, and Scota the ancestress of Malcolm Canmore, Edward I. was himself one of her descendants through Matilda, the daughter of Malcolm and Margaret. Further, when James Stuart, son of Mary Queen of Scots, became King of Great Britain he got the famous stone for his own again and his descendants are still crowned on it in Westminster Abbey.

After Kenneth McAlpine there appears a shadowy son and then a grandson who comes forth into the light at the Battle of Carham in 1018, defeating the King of the Lothians and making the Tweed the boundary between England and Scotland. After some more shadows Duncan and Macbeth stand out in strong relief, for they are known to all the world in Shakespeare's story, and yet shadowy still, for the poet's tale is not history.

Malcolm Canmore is the first King of Scotland that we can call a real historical personage and he is a type of his country at the time he ascended the throne—half-savage still and with the faults and failings of his condition, yet full of noble aspirations and dormant capabilities. We have seen the gentle and kindly side of Malcolm's character in his relations with his beautiful and saintly wife, but there was another and a sterner aspect. It needed a strong man to rule the Scotland that Canmore wrested from Macbeth at Dunsinane, and it was with a strong hand that the victor held it. The wild clansmen of the Highlands feared to rouse his terrible anger and were comparatively peaceful while he reigned, and the Northmen thought twice before they provoked a quarrel with the fierce Scottish king.

The Great Head's anger was, indeed, something to be feared, for he did cruel deeds while it lasted—deeds of blood, that could not be undone in spite of after penitence and remorse. It is sometimes said that St Margaret got all the good things of earth as well as of heaven, but when we dwell on the seamy side of her husband's character, we see hovering over her the shadow of the Cross. The blithe beautiful being who filled the dull rooms of Dunfermline Tower and Edinburgh Castle with life and light and gladness, who was the guardian angel of the poor and wretched, the teacher of all things good and lovely, the nursing-mother of the Church, with whom all things seemed to prosper—happy wife, mother, queen—she had her sorrows, too.

St Margaret had early learnt to suffer in silence, for the sorrows of others had cast their shadow over her in Hungary and also in England. In Scotland, too, long after she had found a home there, she had keen anxieties on account of her brother Edgar Atheling, who continued for years to be an exile and a wanderer. She was torn in two directions, for, while she longed to see her brother King of England, she hated the carnage and bloodshed that attended his attempts to gain the crown.

The descendant of a race of kings and warriors, St Margaret was fearless as any of them, and yet she considered war to be a terrible evil. Peace was necessary for the country she had learned to love as her own, and peace was almost unknown in it. Now to the north, now to the south, King Malcolm sallied forth with fierce elation, to do battle with his own rebels or with Saxon foes, and his wife had to wave her kerchief and bid him God-speed, though her heart was breaking. Afterwards, indeed, weeping before the altar, she bemoaned the deeds of violence that she knew were being done—the sufferings of men, women and children that she was powerless to prevent. God was being offended and she could do nothing but weep for it and offer herself as a victim of expiation.

Her influence with the King was feeble enough when it was a case of war. She indeed never saw his face convulsed with fury as his enemies did. It had ever a look of love and reverence as it turned to her, even when the thought of the coming battle sent the wild blood coursing through his veins. He would smile on her as she remonstrated and would tenderly urge his inability to stop the conflict. Others were the aggressors, perhaps, as in the affair of the men of Moray, and safety depended on prompt action; or it might be that the attack was on her brother's behalf, and surely right and justice were on his side.

Moderation and gentle dealing with the conquered could be promised easily enough, but the Queen knew full well that when Malcolm was beyond the reach of her influence and in one of his fits of ungovernable fury, every promise would be forgotten.

Five times Malcolm invaded England and it is little wonder that English writers depict him as a savage and a barbarian—no less cruel than the heathen Danes of old. His raids were terrible and the gentle giant of Dunfermline was unrecognisable while they lasted. He laid waste the country with fire and sword, slaying without mercy all who crossed his path—men, women and children, "like swine for the banquet" as Simeon of Durham tells of an early invasion. When he spared any, it was to drive them before him to Scotland like a herd of cattle, that they might be parcelled out as slaves among his own subjects. The same Simeon of Durham writes that after one of the Scottish King's raids, "there was not a village, there was not even a house so poor but could boast of some English captive held in thraldom."

St Margaret abhorred slavery and spent large sums of money every year, as we have seen, in setting poor captives free, and yet she had to endure all this. Nay! she had to appear as if she did not see, for duty and love, both made her welcome her husband on his return and rejoice in his victory. It would have been unseemly to meet him with reproaches or weep for his captives at such a time.

Malcolm never had to complain of a cold greeting and so perhaps it was the easier to win him to penitence and pity. Later raids were not so fierce and cruel as the earlier ones, so probably St Margaret's influence had some effect after all.

With wondering admiration and still with a twinkle of humour in his eye at the inconsistency, Malcolm saw the Queen taking his victims under her own special protection, sending them home when it was possible, lightening their burdens when it was not, and giving material help as well as kindly sympathy to all whom she could reach. The Great Head made no objection and did not scruple to give his help when it was required. His fury died out with the end of his raid.

When William the Conqueror had reduced England to something like submission, he resolved to put an end to Canmore's invasions and to teach the Scottish King that a Norman was not to be trifled with. William invaded Scotland with a large army, crossed the Forth and met the Scots at Abernethy. Malcolm's forces were far outnumbered by William's and a battle would have meant crushing defeat for the Scots.

Edgar Atheling, now a pensioner of the Norman King, happily intervened and a conflict was averted. A treaty was signed instead, by which Malcolm promised to disturb English peace no more and to do homage to William for his English territory of Cumberland. It was only owing to the good offices of Edgar Atheling that the Scots obtained such easy terms and they were glad enough when William took his huge army across the Border again.

On this occasion it was scarcely a victory that Malcolm had to report to his anxious Queen, but probably she saw more matter for thanksgiving in it, than she had seen in any of his victories. There was no tale of bloodshed and no train of captives and the treaty just signed promised peace. It was a glorious prospect for poor struggling Scotland which had so long been checked in her growing aspirations by war and its consequent evils.

No parents were ever more blest in their children than Malcolm Canmore and St Margaret, and though the good Queen did not live to see them realise in manhood and womanhood the rich promise of childhood's days, the promise itself was balm to the mother's heart. Here, too, however, there was the shadow of the Cross, for it appears that there was a black sheep in St Margaret's little flock. The story is confused and we cannot get exact details, but it seems that Edmund, the second son of St Margaret, was detected in something like treachery and disloyalty. It must have been serious, for evidently the youth was stripped of his royal rank and right of succession as a punishment. It is good to hear that he repented and did penance, for Wynton and Fordun speak of him as a "man of gret wertu" and other writers tell us that he died a monk in the monastery of Montacute, in Somersetshire.

The unfaithful son had no doubt been led away by bad companions, and yet we hear of little actual opposition to Malcolm and Margaret. There were occasional growlings indeed in the north and west from some of the old Celts who were jealous of the growing Saxon influence, and Donald Bane, Malcolm's younger brother, was ready to take advantage of any unrest on his own behalf as soon as an opportunity would show itself. It is possible that Donald had in some way got his young nephew into his power and so led him astray.

The Celtic chiefs had some reason for discontent. They saw their beloved Gaelic give place to Saxon at the court of their king, Celt though he was, and beheld all the places of honour there filled by Saxon men and women. The country south of the Forth and Clyde had been to them as a foreign land and now it was attaining to greater importance than their beloved Caledonia itself. Their hearts were sore at the supposed slight given to their dear mountains and at the loss of their own ascendancy. The feeling, however, was not strong enough for rebellion and would probably have expended itself only in wild outbursts of wrath against individual Sassenachs as it has often done since, but for the ambitious aspirations of Donald Bane.

There is no evidence whatever of any antipathy to the fair Saxon Queen. In the depths of these rugged Celtic hearts there was admiration for her beauty and reverence for her goodness and appreciation of the kindness which she bestowed impartially on Celt and Saxon. Malcolm indeed was blamed often enough for forgetting his old friends, and Celtic mutterings sometimes reached even to the court. These occasioned the good Queen anxiety and sorrow for she would fain have seen Celt and Saxon, united in one people, laying aside race rivalries and working together for their country's good.

St Margaret was sometimes accorded glimpses into the future. Did she see the wonderful change that the coming ages would bring about? Who would have dreamt in the eleventh century of a time when the descendants of St Margaret, driven from the throne by the Saxons themselves, would find their staunchest allies and firmest friends among the Celts?

CHAPTER 14

Margaret's Last Years

In the last years of her life St Margaret had to endure much bodily suffering. Her constant labours, her watchings, her abstinence and austerities had worn out a body never too robust and she seems to have fallen into a lingering consumption.

No illness, however, could impair the sweet strength of her soul, and it was only when the increasing weakness of her poor body told its own secret that those around began to realise that something was amiss. Still she abated nothing of her prayer and pious reading, her almsgiving and other works of mercy. Her pains and failing strength were borne as if unnoticed, and her attendants marvelled at their Queen's courage and tranquillity as they saw her wasting away before their eyes from day to day.

Gradually her journeys became fewer and shorter as she found herself less and less capable of exertion. Her last journey must have been from Dunfermline to Edinburgh, for she died in the Maidens' Castle, and one of her confessors tells that for six months before the period of her last illness she was unable to mount a horse.

Though the good Queen disregarded her sufferings she recognised to what they tended, but death has no terrors for those whose lives have been spent in God's service.

"She willingly accepted," says her chronicler, "with patience and thanksgiving the pains of the flesh, regarding them as the stripes of a most loving Father."

As she grew weaker St Margaret began to live in the thoughts of heaven and to detach herself more and more from earthly things and people. It was not a hard task for one who had always lived "in the world but not of it." She had worked with all her strength while it was day, and now, as her night drew near, she thirsted after death, saying often, in the words of the *Psalmist—*

My soul hath thirsted after the strong living God; when shall I come and appear before the Face of God.

Her children and friends hoped against hope and dared not think of court and country without her. King Malcolm, intent on his quarrels with William Rufus, seems not to have realised that his wife was dying. Her weakness was so gradual in its coming that he probably grew accustomed to it and forgot the vigour of former days, and then, there was never a murmur or a complaint to suggest to him that this weakness was the effect of suffering. As to the Queen herself it does not seem to have occurred to her that her death would be a calamity for her family and country. She was but an instrument in God's hands, and He could work through others when her heart had ceased to beat.

Turgot parted with St Margaret nearly a year before her death. Perhaps she left him at Dunfermline, but more probably he was obliged to pay a lengthy visit to Durham Abbey, of which he afterwards became Prior.

"It would seem," says this holy man, "that her departure from the world and certain other events which were impending had been known to her beforehand."

It is certain that St Margaret was convinced that she was parting from her old friend forever. A great sadness weighed her down as arrangements were made for his going, and finally she summoned him to her and with sighs and tears of compunction made to him a general confession of her whole life. The holy man wept with her, marvelling at her close union with God and judging himself unworthy to be associated with one so holy in such sacred relationship. At last the parting came and both the Queen and her confessor wept anew. For twenty-four years they had known each other intimately and helped each other in the service of God, and both knew that their next meeting would be in heaven.

"I now bid you farewell," said the Queen. "I shall not continue much longer in this world, but you will live after me a considerable time. There are two things which I beg of you. One is that as long as you survive you will remember me in your prayers; the other is that you will take some care about my sons and daughters. Lavish your affection on them; teach them above all things to love and fear God.

"When you see any of them exalted to the height of an earthly dignity, then at once, his father and his master in the truest sense, go to him, warn him, lest, through a passing honour, he become puffed up with pride or offend God by avarice, or through prosperity in this world forget the blessedness of the life which is eternal."

Turgot promised through his tears to obey her wishes in all things and they parted as St Margaret had foreseen never to meet again on earth.

After the Queen's death Turgot became Prior of Durham Abbey and in 1199, when her son Alexander was King of Scotland, the Prior was consecrated Archbishop of St Andrew's.

St Margaret's work was finished and she knew it. Her farewell to Turgot was her last will and testament and now she had only to wait a little longer and to be purified by suffering, that so having drunk to the dregs of her Lord's chalice, she might be ready at His call to enter into His glory.

CHAPTER 15

Margaret's Death

When William the Conqueror died, he was succeeded by his son William Rufus. This prince had never approved of Cumberland being a Scottish dependency, and as soon as he found himself in power, he resolved to wrest from Malcolm Canmore every foot of land which that King possessed south of the Sol way.

Rufus built a strong castle at Carlisle and made other warlike preparations. Canmore soon heard of these doings, and he, too, began to make preparations, for he was just as determined to keep Cumberland as the English King was to take it. He would invade Northumberland at once and punish Rufus for breaking the Conqueror's treaty.

Meantime, the Queen was in Edinburgh Castle with her children. Edward and Edgar were splendid princes, stalwart and handsome and both distinguished by a nobility of character that promised well for the Scotland of the future if they were destined to rule over it. Edward had already reached man's estate and was eager to follow his father to battle, and Edgar, though ever a lover of peace, had plenty of courage and would not be left behind, stripling though he was. Edmund had disappeared from the royal family circle before this crisis and Ethelred, the third son, was also gone. One chronicler speaks of him as being at a later date Abbot of Dunkeld and the only thing further that history tells is that he was buried with his holy mother in Dunfermline Abbey Church.

St Margaret's health had failed considerably before the quarrel with William Rufus began, and the anxiety she had to endure while her husband made his terrible preparations, told severely on her weakened frame. All her sweet buoyancy of spirit was gone and for the first time in her life the depression and mental anguish she suffered made itself apparent to others. For once she offered a prolonged opposition to

Malcolm's design and pleaded with him to stay at home and let Rufus work his will with Cumberland. The poor Queen's expostulations were useless. In spite of "much dissuading," King Malcolm persevered in his determination, tenderly telling his wife that illness had made her over-anxious. When she saw that the King's determination was too strong to be shaken St Margaret implored that at least her sons might be left with her. It was all in vain. The boys must learn to act like men and princes, said their father, but it was only a matter of a few days or weeks. The Queen should ere long welcome them all three home again with banners flying and a glorious tale of victory.

St Margaret was neither persuaded nor consoled, for her soul was dark with premonitions of coming evil, but she had to acquiesce in her husband's arrangements. As usual her submission was whole-hearted. Her own hands, weak as they were, embroidered the King's banner and she was on the walls surrounded by her maidens and children to wave a last farewell.

Anxious days followed, during which the poor sick Queen eagerly looked for news of her dear ones. Riders had, of course, to be sent back with messages and it seemed to the waiting wife and mother that they were few and slow in coming. On former occasions it had been hard enough to think of her husband in danger, but now there were her two young sons as well—the hope of Scotland. They were but children still in their anxious mother's eyes and they were all untried in the terrible game of war. And then—cruel remembrance—the enemy was of no alien race. The Scots had gone to fight against her own kindred, for though the leaders of the English armies were Normans, the soldiers were for the most part Saxon.

The November of 1093 was like the ordinary November familiar to Edinburgh people, dull and cheerless, with leaden skies and dreary drizzling rain. The weather aggravated the Queen's malady but she strove to continue her daily duties and was only very reluctantly induced to give up some of her penitential exercises. She dragged herself to Mass each morning in her chapel on the summit of the cliff, though often she was so weak that she had almost to be carried back to her chamber, and she prayed unceasingly.

Troubles multiplied themselves in those gloomy days. Rumours soon reached the Castle that another enemy had risen up against the poor Queen and her children, more unnatural still than the English. Donald Bane, Malcolm's brother, at the head of a band of malcontents, stirred up by himself for purposes of ambition, was holding himself

St Margarets Chapel, Edinburgh Castle.

ready to take advantage of any mishap on the English frontier.

Ill as she was, the Queen spent hours in her chapel after this news came. Prostrate before the altar she implored God's protection for her husband, children and people in the terrible trial that had befallen Scotland. Her own life was well-nigh over but she trembled for the fate of her four helpless children left to the mercies of their vindictive uncle, should anything go amiss in England.

In God she placed all her trust, but it was her hour of desolation, and even in prayer, trials were not wanting. There at the altar, where she had always found relief in communing with her Lord, and courage to bear anxiety and disappointment with tranquillity, she knelt now, dry and cold and unconsoled. The sweet sense of His presence was gone and she felt utterly alone. She had desired to suffer with Christ and in her last days especially He allowed her to taste of the bitterness of His Chalice and even to know something of the awful mental anguish that wrung from Him on the cross the mysterious words "*My God, my God, why hast Thou forsaken Me.*"

Strange gleams of the future and of distant happenings came to St Margaret in this prayer of desolation, and she who had always borne sorrow and pain with such sweet fortitude was weighed down with sadness and trouble. Her attendants scarcely knew how to act in the strange circumstances. Their gentle mistress had always been their comforter and now she required comfort from them. They thronged round her begging that she would take some repose and spare her poor weak body and they spoke hopefully of the speedy return of the King and the end of all their anxieties. Their mistress thanked them graciously, as was her custom, for their love and thoughtfulness but would not join in their hopeful talk of the future.

Presently the Queen's confessor came to talk with her and when he spoke of the King and the army, St Margaret gently laid her hand on his and said in clear low tones as if speaking to herself rather than to him:—

Perhaps, today, a great evil has fallen on the Scots, such as has not happened to them for many ages past.

Astonishment and fear took hold of the little group of children and attendants. The listeners had fathers, husbands or brothers with the King and a chill came on their hearts as the Queen spoke, but they still strove to be cheerful and told their royal mistress that anxiety and bodily suffering made her exaggerate evil possibilities. St Margaret only smiled sadly and returned to the chapel to pray.

Meanwhile, Malcolm was ravaging Northumbria in his usual fashion when he met his death suddenly and unexpectedly. The ancient story tells that he laid siege to Alnwick and that the Northumbrians, knowing the Great Head of old and despairing of holding out against him, proposed submission. A certain Norman knight, however, thought of a stratagem for ridding Alnwick of its great enemy. They would indeed offer submission but the keys would only be delivered to the Scottish King in person and he must come to the gates to receive them.

Nothing loth, Malcolm appeared before the gates without delay and then the Norman knight, pretending to present the keys on a spear, by a sudden movement turned the weapon on the King of Scots and pierced his eye. The spear penetrated the brain and Malcolm fell back dead while the successful Norman returning to his comrades bore ever after the name of Pierce-eye or Percy.

Many of us learnt this tale in history in the days of our youth and yet it appears to be but a legend. Mr Freeman says that Malcolm's death occurred near the spot known as Malcolm's Cross, from a road erected there in memory of the dead King. The ruins of a chapel are still to be seen at Malcolm's Cross—another relic of the care that his children had for his soul. The River Alne separates this ground from the town of Alnwick and so the old story cannot be even approximately true. By a stratagem, Freeman tells us, which even English writers consider treacherous, Earl Robert of Mowbray led his forces against the King of Scots. "Malcolm was killed and with him died his son and expected heir, Edward. The actual slayer of Malcom was his gossip Morel, Earl Robert's nephew and steward."

The Alne was swollen by heavy rains and, in the confusion that followed Canmore's death, those of his army who escaped English swords perished in the flooded river. Two natives put King Malcolm's body on a cart and it was buried for the time being at Tynemouth.

With only a miserable remnant of his father's gallant army, Prince Edgar returned to Scotland. It was a gloomy march and the poor boy had a sad tale of disaster to tell at the end of it. Sorrow awaited him, too. As he approached Edinburgh Castle his mother lay dying within its walls.

It was four days since she had spoken the words that had so terrified her attendants. She seemed stronger and on this 16th day of November she went to her oratory to Mass as usual. "And there" says the priest who attended her these last days "she took care to provide herself beforehand, for her departure was now near, with the Holy Viaticum of the Body and Blood of Our Lord."

On returning to her chamber St Margaret became so ill that it was evident to all death was at hand. Her body began to grow cold, her face was ghastly pale, and the sweat of death was on her brow. The royal children and the Queen's maidens knelt around her couch, weeping bitterly, She spoke to them lovingly and blessed them with her feeble hand, but she retained her composure and begged her chaplain and the other priests present to pray for her departing soul.

Presently she asked for her great treasure the Black Rood of Scotland. For this image of her Saviour St Margaret had a special love because it contained a portion of the true Cross "as has been proved by convincing miracles," says Aelred. Only the case was black, for the cross itself was of pure gold and set with diamonds of great size and beauty. Queen Margaret herself had brought it to Scotland and her sons afterwards treasured it as a precious relic of their saintly mother. David I. placed it in Holy rood Abbey where it remained until the invasion of Edward I. who carried it with many other Scottish treasures to England. Robert the Bruce demanded its restoration with such vehemence that Queen Isabella, the mother of Edward III., yielded it up to him when the Treaty of Independence was signed during her regency in 1327. The English were furious and could more easily have pardoned the Regent for her great misdeeds than for her complaisance in this instance.

St Margaret's attendants had some difficulty in opening the chest which contained the Black Rood and the dying Queen sighed deeply at the delay.

"Unhappy and guilty that I am," she said softly to herself; "shall I not be permitted to look once more on the Holy Cross."

At last the crucifix was placed in her trembling hands and she looked at it long and lovingly, signing herself with it from time to time and murmuring tender ejaculations as she kissed the sacred wounds. Presently with a great effort she raised it in both hands and looking at the crucified figure steadfastly repeated in a clear voice the whole of the "*Miserere*." The poor weak hands soon sank down again, but still they held the crucifix and still the Saint prayed earnestly though life was ebbing fast away.

Around the Castle was an intense silence. The clouds hung in the sky like gloomy curtains and no breath of wind stirred the branches of the forest trees. The sentinels shivered and were conscious of something weird and eerie in the stillness. Within the death-chamber there was the unceasing murmur of prayer. The priests were recommending the departing soul to God and the Queen's voice, very weak now, was firmly joining in the responses. The royal children and the Queen's maidens had given up trying to join in the prayers and were weeping quietly.

Suddenly the outside silence was broken. The blast of a horn resounded from beyond the walls and was answered by the warder at the gates. It was a royal messenger with tidings of the King and the army. Something seemed to warn the sad group round St Margaret's bed that the news would be better untold, but while they framed the wish in their hearts that the Queen might be kept in ignorance of the messenger's arrival Prince Edgar entered the room.

The poor boy was travel-stained and weary. His heart was heavy with sorrow at the loss of his father and brother and the defeat of the gallant Scottish army. He was overwhelmed, moreover, with the thought of the immense responsibility that had fallen on his young shoulders for ill news travels fast and he had heard on his way home of the warlike preparations of his uncle Donald Bane.

Edgar knew that his mother was ill and entered her chamber resolving to tell his evil tidings gently. He loved her dearly and his only hope amidst his terrible difficulties was the thought that he could look to her for counsel and help. The shock was unspeakable when he saw her lying, as was evident, at the point of death. His message was forgotten and anguish such as he had not yet known welled up in his heart, till he felt that it must break. With the ready hopefulness of youth, he had looked on his mother's ill-health as but a passing ailment, but now he knew the truth. With a low moan he sank on his knees by the Queen's bed and burst into tears.

St Margaret had been lying still and silent since the horn sounded, and she seemed unconscious of what was passing around, but suddenly she rallied and looking on Edgar with wonderful calmness and no apparent surprise asked for news of his father and brother.

"They are well," faltered the boy, fearing that if he were to tell her suddenly of their death she, too, would die. She sighed deeply and placed her thin hand lovingly on her son's bent head and then she spoke again.

"I know it, my boy, I know it" she said. "And now, by this Holy Cross, by the bond of our blood, I adjure you, Edgar, to tell me the truth. How fares it with the King and my Edward?"

The prince attempted no more concealment.

"The King and Edward are both slain," he said, and in a voice broken by weeping he told the story of the treachery of the English and his brave father's death.

The boy's recital was often interrupted by the sobs of the children and attendants, but the Queen heard it in silence with her hands and eyes raised to heaven.

Gradually it dawned on all present excepting Prince Edgar that the Queen was hearing no news. She had seen in vision the death of her husband and first-born son. As the youth told the day and hour of his father's death, they recalled the prophetic words that had so startled them four days earlier:—

Perhaps today a great evil has fallen on the Scots, such as has not happened to them for many ages past.

When the dying Queen had heard her son to the end, she remained for a short space rapt in silent prayer and then she said aloud:—

"All praise be to Thee, Almighty God, who hast been pleased that I should endure such deep sorrow at my departing, and I trust that by means of this suffering, it is Thy pleasure that I should be cleansed from the stains of my sins."

Death was very near now and St Margaret knew it. Once more she looked lovingly at each dear face around her bed and strove to raise her feeble hand in blessing. It was the poor mother's last farewell. Presently she began the prayer uttered by the priest in the Mass, before He receives the Body and Blood of Christ.

"Lord Jesus Christ," she prayed, "Who, according to the will of the Father, through the co-operation of the Holy Ghost, hast by Thy death given life to the world, deliver me."

As she uttered the words "Deliver me" her pure soul was indeed delivered from the prison of the body "and departed to Christ, the Author of true liberty."

Thus died the saintly Margaret, Princess of Hungary and England, and Queen of Scotland, on 16th November, 1093, in the forty-eighth year of her age.

The account of her holy death was given to Turgot by the priest who assisted her on her death-bed and who was probably the Theodoric, so often confused with Turgot. "She loved him "says the latter "more intimately than the others on account of his simplicity and innocence."

The priest, on his part, was so affected by the Queen's holiness and so touched by her death that he became a monk in the Abbey of Durham and offered his sacrifice for the repose of her soul.

When the Queen was dead, the ghastly pallor left her, and with it the traces of the anguish and pain that she had suffered in her last hour. Her sweet face was serene and tranquil in death and suffused with fair and warm hues so that as those who saw her reported—"It seemed as if she were not dead but sleeping."

For centuries after the Queen's death her room was preserved pretty much as she left it. In the days of the early Stewarts it was still known as "The Blessed Margaret's Chamber."

CHAPTER 16

Margaret's Burial

History has little to say of the career of Donald Bane or the Fair-haired, during the lifetime of Malcolm Canmore. Shakespeare tells that he fled to Ireland when his father Duncan was murdered, and we do not hear his name in connection with Malcolm's successful attack on Dunsinane. It appears that he came seldom, if ever, to court and that disaffected Celts might always count on his sympathy. His whereabouts were uncertain and vague suggestions of impending evil came with his name, and so he hovered about among the mountains like a bird of ill-omen, waiting for his opportunity.

Many a time he had seen his brother go south with banners flying and had looked and hoped for news of disaster, only to hear instead the wild shouts of triumph that greeted the returning victor.

In 1093 Donald had organised quite an extensive conspiracy, for at last Fate seemed to favour his designs. The Queen, whose influence he knew and feared, was ill—perhaps dying. The King had gone to fight against great odds, and with him were all his most devoted friends and followers and also his eldest son Edward, regarded generally as the heir of Scotland.

It does not appear that Donald Bane's contingent of Celts was a strong one in spite of race jealousies, but here, too, Fate favoured the adventurer. Malcolm Canmore had in this last year of his reign ceded the Western Isles again to the King of Norway. His reason for doing so is not clear, but he may have thought that his English enterprise was enough for the time being, and Cumberland was certainly more valuable than the Hebrides. Whatever his reasons, the result showed itself at once in a great influx of Northmen, and Donald Bane resolved to attach them to himself. He appealed to the King of Norway for help and promised him in the event of success all the Western Islands that were not already his, including Bute and Arran. Donald thus found himself at the head of a considerable army mainly composed of hordes of Norwegians and half-savage clansmen from Bute and the Islands.

No sooner was Queen Margaret dead than consternation spread abroad among the inmates of the Castle. Donald Bane, whose very name they dreaded, was at the gates and clamouring for admittance. The fortress was strong and the enemy might indeed be kept out for a long time, but hunger would compel them to admit him eventually and then. . . . Woe to the royal children! There was little doubt but that Donald Bane, once admitted, would follow the ancient savage usage and sweep his helpless nephews and nieces remorselessly from his path.

He was not to reach them, however. The good Queen had still a care for her children, and was watching over them from Heaven. All within the Castle walls were faithful and true, and so brief councils were held and followed by speedy action. The assailants were at the gates only, on the eastern side of the fortress, for they evidently considered escape on any other side a sheer impossibility. Suddenly the air became hazy and a "great myst" crept up from the sea, enveloping rock and forest in its clammy embrace. Those who are acquainted with Edinburgh mists and Edinburgh Castle cliffs will scarcely be surprised that Donald Bane considered them safe custodians for his poor little prisoners and intended victims. Besides, the inmates of the Castle were mainly priests, women and children, and it was unseemly that great warriors should waste time and strategy on such weak enemies. Better far to assemble in full force before the gates, to effect an entrance by striking terror to the hearts of those within and then to work their will.

"*Man proposes—but God disposes*," and He also helps the weak who trust in Him. While the besiegers battered at the gates, the body of St Margaret, "shrouded as became a Queen," was carried through a postern on the west and lowered with reverence and care down the great wall of rock. Somehow—for the tale has never been told in detail, the royal children and their attendants followed, and when at last Donald Bane effected an entrance to the fortress, his prey had flown.

The "great myst" for which the fugitives thanked God as for something miraculous covered their flight down the cliffs and through the forest to the Queen's Ferry. True, a mist in November is no great miracle in Edinburgh as modern writers take care to point out, but that of 1093 helped the royal children and their protectors as effectively as if their enemies had been struck blind, and the providence of God is shown by little things as well as by great. The children of St Margaret had been taught to seek God's help in all things, and there was nothing remarkable in their thinking that He sent the "great myst" specially for them.

It seems, indeed, more remarkable, that the mist helped instead, of hindering them. The Castle rock is not an inviting stair in broad daylight and a clear atmosphere, and the fugitives came down in the misty dusk and yet they were unscathed. They made their way, too, through the gloomy woods and across the Forth to loyal Fife. It was a sorrowful little party—the dead Queen carried by her faithful friends, the little children deprived within the last few days of father, brother and mother, and poor Edgar, now the head of the family and but a boy himself. The priest who directed the undertaking did a wonderful thing in carrying out his plan so successfully.

The wild men of Argyle and Bute were lurking among the forest trees like beasts of prey, but they saw nothing save the white mist and heard nothing but the distant murmur of the sea. Thus in secret, hidden by the darkness and the mist, was St Margaret's sacred body borne across the sea to Dunfermline and buried in the Church of the Holy Trinity, which she herself had built. There, says her chaplain, it was committed to the grave, "opposite the altar and the venerable sign of the Holy Cross which she had erected."

Before the rude altar with honour
She was laid in holy sepulchre;
There her lord was laid also;
And with them their sons two,
Edward the First and Ethelred.

So the story is told in Wynton's chronicle. It was not, however, until twenty years later that Malcolm's remains were brought to rest with those of his Queen. He was buried as we have seen at Tynemouth in 1093, but in 1115 his son Alexander I., then King of Scotland, had his body and that of Prince Edward carried back to Scotland and buried in Dunfermline. David I., St Margaret's youngest son, who covered Scottish land with churches and abbeys, almost rebuilt the sacred edifice erected by his parents. By the time he came to the throne, Durham cathedral had risen in all its beauty and had probably suggested to the King the form of the splendid structure which he raised in honourable memory of his illustrious parents.

A hundred years later Alexander II. made further additions and improvements and the beautiful abbey church remained much as he left it until the destructive days of the Reformation.

In 1250 Queen Margaret was solemnly canonised by Pope Innocent IV., but she had been canonised by public opinion for one hundred and fifty years before that date. As the people had loved her and sought her help in life, so their children honoured her and sought her help after her death. In the centuries that followed, when her sons were building up a splendid Scotland on the foundations she had laid, men and women spoke of and trusted in the "good Queen" as if she had been a living friend of unlimited resources and also of unlimited goodwill. The simple Scots of Catholic days brought all their troubles great and small to St Margaret's tomb, and when help and comfort came in answer to their prayers there was ever a heartfelt "Thanks to God and the good Queen." St Margaret's body had not been long in the Church of the Holy Trinity when the poor found their way to her grave, and wonderful stories were told of favours granted to these unfortunates who were evidently the Queen's favourites in death as they had been in life. They had never been sent away empty-handed from her palace doors, nor were they from her tomb.

It was from these poor ones kneeling beside their dear Saint's remains that a tale first came of an exquisite shimmering silvery light that hovered over the Queen's grave and filled the church with a soft radiance. Great numbers saw it at different times and were strangely moved, so that they felt constrained to make their peace with God and to strive after greater sanctity of life in future.

On 19th June, 1250, the year in which her canonisation took place, St Margaret's body was taken from its first resting-place and placed in a silver shrine, richly adorned with precious stones. In the newly built "Lady Aisle" a splendid receptacle had been prepared for the shrine. It consisted of a double plinth of marble from the upper of which rose "six slender shafts of shapely stone," supporting a highly ornamented canopy. Under this canopy the shrine was to stand. There is yet one legend to be told in connection with St Margaret, and it has reference to the translation of her relics.

The new shrine was prepared and the Abbey Church of Dunfermline was filled to overflowing with a devout congregation all eager to do honour to St Margaret, whose dear name had at last been added to the glorious roll of the saints of Mother Church. When the grave was opened a delicate fragrance as of sweet-smelling flowers came forth from the sacred remains, filling the church and delighting those present. Reverently the privileged bearers raised the body of the Saint and the procession moved onward towards the Lady Aisle. But behold a marvel! As the procession reached the spot where rested the body of Malcolm Canmore, brought back from Northumbria, something went amiss. The bearers of the Queen's body felt their sacred burden suddenly grow heavy as lead and were obliged to rest it on the ground. Aid was immediately forthcoming, but it was of no avail, and consternation filled the church. Presently a voice was heard and an old monk, himself near death, was seen standing with his trembling hand extended towards St Margaret's body.

"The Queen desires," he said in shaking accents, "that in death her husband should share her honours as in life she shared his."

It was an age of faith, and marvels of this kind were scarce considered marvellous. Without more ado other bearers were summoned and told to raise the body of King Malcolm and place it beside that of his Queen. It was done, and lo! the Queen's body, now light as a feather, was easily carried to its beautiful resting-place.

Poor, faulty Malcolm! It was thus through her whom he had loved and reverenced so much on earth, that he gained after death an honour to which of himself he had small title. Who shall doubt that St Margaret's intercession had already brought his soul through purgatorial fires to share her bliss in Heaven?

From 1250 to 1560 lights were kept perpetually burning before St Margaret's shrine and frequent mention is made in the ancient registers of Dunfermline of donations given for this purpose. For three hundred years the abbey church was a place of pilgrimage, and grateful Scottish hearts poured out thanks to God for favours granted at her shrine, and through her intercession. When John Knox's followers were abroad, spreading the "pure Gospel" by destruction and plunder, the faithful Catholics feared the remains of their beloved Saint and patron would be treated with contumely, and so they secretly removed them, The Reformers came, and finding the treasure gone, revenged themselves by expending their fury on the marble tomb, breaking into fragments the pillars and canopy that their ancestors had so lovingly fashioned for the good Queen. The double plinth of marble resisted their hammers and it may still be seen in the churchyard of Dunfermline Abbey.

When the relics of St Margaret were carried away from Dunfermline Abbey, the head with its long fair hair was brought to Mary Queen

St Margaret's Tomb

of Scots, then in Edinburgh. After her flight to England, a Benedictine monk had the relic in his keeping for a long time, and from his hands it passed into those of the Jesuits. Finally it was translated to the Scots College, Donay, and was seen there in 1785, still with its fair hair in wonderful preservation. It disappeared during the confusion of the French Revolution. Other portions of the holy Queen's relics were given to Philip II., King of Spain, and placed by him in the Church of St Lawrence at the Escurial. During the Pontificate of Pius IX. the bishops of Scotland asked for permission to bring these relics to Scotland in order that their beloved Saint might again be duly honoured in the country of her adoption. The permission was readily granted, but the relics could not be found or, at all events, identified. Thus it happens that no part of St Margaret's sacred body is known to be in the country where she wore an earthly and won a heavenly crown.

St Margaret died on November 16th, and for nearly three hundred years after her canonisation the Church kept her feast on that day. During the turbulent days of the Reformation there was a change and the reason for it is not clear. The 10th of June was substituted for the 16th of November. Mary of Guise, the mother of Mary Queen of Scots died on the 10th of June and as the faithful Catholics of Scotland regarded this Queen-Regent as a saint, some writers assign this as a reason for the change. After the Union of the Crowns the few who still kept the feast seem to have returned to the ancient date, but in the eighteenth century June 10th is again St Margaret's Day. James Stuart, the old Pretender, had a great devotion to the Saint, and he preferred the 10th of June because it happened to be his own birthday. He was exiled and lonely, and the Pope—thus Highlanders tell the story— changed the date of the feast to give him pleasure. There were few Scottish Catholics left then to be interested or to make objections.

For nearly two hundred years St Margaret's Feast was kept on June 10th, but when, a few years ago, there was a thorough revision of the Scottish Calendar, it was decided to place the feast on the day of the holy Queen's death.

Throughout Scotland the feast of St Margaret is now kept on November 16th. It is held in great esteem by Scottish Catholics, and we hope and pray that a time is coming when the great and good Queen will be known and loved as she ought to be in the country of her adoption and when her feast will again be a red-letter day in Scotland as it was before the Reformation.

CHAPTER 17

Margaret's Children

While Donald Bane was making sure of his position in Edinburgh and striving to maintain something like order among the ill-assorted divisions of his army, the good Queen's burial had quietly been effected in Dunfermline and the royal children were safely over the Border before their uncle had time to give them more of his attention.

Edgar Atheling seems at this period to have possessed both position and influence in England for he was able to protect his three nephews, to provide for the suitable completion of the education of the younger ones, and finally to assist Edgar to ascend the throne of Scotland.

The young princesses, Matilda and Mary, were conducted to the Convent where their aunt, Princess Christina, was now Prioress. They had been carefully educated by their saintly mother, and were refined and accomplished, as well as virtuous and beautiful maidens. The Prioress took care that her sister's work should be suitably completed and both St Margaret's daughters proved worthy children of such a mother. Princess Matilda was especially beautiful, and to save her from the unwelcome attentions of the rough young nobles whom she was occasionally obliged to meet, her prudent aunt insisted on her wearing a veil like those of the nuns. The Princess strongly objected, and, as she had a decided will of her own, there were some comparatively stormy interviews between herself and the Prioress. It was no question of being a nun. Both Princesses were devoted to piety and works of charity, as might have been expected of St Margaret's daughters, but neither showed any inclination for the religious life, and this the Prioress recognised.

Henry I. of England sought the hand of Princess Matilda in marriage presently, and with the approval of the Prioress and the brothers of the young Princess an engagement was entered on. No marriage could have been more suitable, for it united the ancient dynasty and the new, but Norman jealousy was excited at the prospect and the barons of the new order tried their best to prevent the union. As no other objection could be thought of, they declared that the Princess "had been veiled" in the convent and was not free to marry.

Matilda herself explained how and why she had been "veiled" and declared that she had never taken vows or thought of taking them, knowing as she did that God had not called her to a religious life. The Prioress upheld her niece, and St Anselm not only declared Princess Matilda free to marry, but performed the marriage ceremony himself, and crowned St Margaret's eldest daughter as Queen of England.

This incident is often a stumbling-block to writers who do not understand religious vocation. The attitude of the Princess showed no disrespect either to the convent or to religion, but simply the deter- mination not to be forced by accidental circumstances into a life for which she had no inclination. Never had England a better Queen! As a child she had been associated with her saintly mother in her works of mercy and charity, and had been taught by example as well as by precept that a Queen should be as a mother to the poor and wretched. In her high station Matilda lost no time in showing how well she had profited by St Margaret's lessons. Her spirit of penance and prayer was scarcely less remarkable than that of her holy mother, she was a de- voted friend to priests and religions, encouraging them to be zealous for the good of the Church and helping them by rich gifts, and she was so kind and good to the poor and so winning and affable in her intercourse with people of every rank that she was devotedly loved by all, and spoken of during her life and after her death as "the good Queen Maud."

Mary, the younger Princess, married Eustace, Count of Boulogne, and her daughter also became Queen of England for she married Stephen, the nephew of Henry I.

As has been already told, three of St Margaret's sons became in turn Kings of Scotland. Donald Bane indeed succeeded in his attempt to seize the supreme power at Malcolm's death, but his reign was short and stormy. Prince Duncan, Malcolm Canmore's son by his first wife, had been given to William the Conqueror as a hostage to ensure the fidelity of the Scottish King to the pledges of Abernethy, and so had grown to manhood in England. William Rufus knew Duncan well, and preferring him to Donald Bane as a neighbour, he sent him north with an army to take the Crown from his uncle. Donald Bane was defeated and Duncan became King, but his reign, like the preceding one, was brief and troubled. Donald Bane reappeared, and according to some authorities brought with him Edmund, the unfaithful son of St Margaret. Duncan was killed in a somewhat mysterious manner, and Donald Bane again assumed the kingship, dividing his territory with Edmund.

Celts and Saxons, however, were weary of anarchy and war, and began to realise better, how much good St Margaret had done, by contrasting her times with the troubled years since her death.

William Rufus still had strong objections to Donald Bane as a neighbouring sovereign, and Edgar Atheling was active in rousing English sympathy on behalf of his nephew Edgar, who had now reached man's estate. Edgar had no love for war, but he had plenty of courage when the necessity showed itself, and on this occasion, the chroniclers tell us, he was encouraged by dreams and visions, urging him to proceed and promising victory. As his army marched northward across the country between the Solway and the Forth, St Cuthbert appeared to him in glory and said solemnly:—"Fear nothing, Edgar; God has given thee the victory."

And so it happened. Victory was easy and complete. Donald Bane disappeared from the pages of history, and Edgar, the son of St Margaret, became King of Scotland. Edgar the Peaceable and Alexander the Fierce had both their share in the making of Scotland, but it was David the Saint, the good Queen's youngest son, who did most for Church and State. We have seen how he "illumined the land," as an ancient writer says, "with kirks and with abbeys," and also how he won for himself the title of "protector of the poor." When he marched into England to support the claim of his niece Matilda against the usurper Stephen, his army, gathered from all parts of Scotland, shows how strong was his hold on that land of many peoples. There were Highlanders as well as Lowlanders in his army, and also the wild warriors of Bute and Argyle.

The Galloway men were there too, and lastly a body of Norman knights who had settled in Scotland. David was defeated at Northallerton, but he was able to rally his forces before he reached the Border, and Stephen was glad enough to buy him off by giving him the counties of Northumberland and Cumberland. King David spent the last years of his life for the most part at Carlisle and died there in 1153. One morning at dawn he was found in his room on his knees "with his two hands joined together on his breast and raised to heaven." His attendants thought at first that he was rapt in prayer, but he was dead.

For two hundred years the direct descendants of St Margaret ruled over Scotland and this is the happiest period in its history. It took an honourable place among the nations of Europe and flourished exceedingly.

Churches, monasteries and schools appeared all over the country, good laws were made and kept, commerce grew apace, industries prospered and towns sprang up in the neighbourhood of every navigable river. Forests were cut down and cultivated fields took their place. The people had everywhere plenty to do, and soon became prosperous and happy. The reign of Alexander III. was especially a "Golden Age" for Scotland. The Northmen were ousted forever and peace and order ruled the land. St Margaret's methods had proved successful and there were no longer crowds of destitute and starving poor to be fed and clothed. There was work for all who were able to do it, and the monks took care of those who could not work. Improvements and progress went on with scarce a check until the doubly dark night in 1286 when the horse of Alexander III. stumbled and fell with its rider over the Kinghorn cliffs.

Margaret, the Maid of Norway, the heiress of Scotland, died two years after her grandfather, and her death brought on Scotland the long and harassing war of Scottish Independence.

Four of St Margaret's sons are buried in Dunfermline Abbey, and with them lies Duncan, their half-brother. Iona had been a place of royal sepulture, but, with St Margaret's burial, Dunfermline took its place, and many kings and queens lie there awaiting the dread summons, "*Arise ye dead and come to Judgment.*" The last King of Scotland buried in Dunfermline was Robert the Bruce.

CHAPTER 18

St Margaret, Patron of Scotland

"The path of a good woman," says Ruskin, "is indeed strewn with flowers; but they rise behind her steps, not before them.

Her feet have touched the meadows and left the daisies rosy.

"You think that only a lover's fancy? How if it could be true? You think this also perhaps only a poet's fancy:

E'en the slight harebell raised its head
Elastic, from her airy tread.

"But it is little to say of a woman that she only does not destroy as she passes; she should revive; the harebells should bloom, not stoop as she passes. I mean what I say in calm English. You have heard it said that flowers only flourish rightly in the garden of one who loves them. I know you would like that to be true. You would think it a pleasant magic if you could flush your flowers into brighter bloom by a kind look upon them; nay more, if your look had the power not only to cheer but to guard; if you could bid the black blight turn away and the knotted caterpillar spare if you could bid the dew fall upon them in the drought and say to the south wind in frost, 'Come, thou south wind, and breathe upon my garden.' This you would think a great thing, and is it not a greater thing that all this you can do for fairer flowers than these—flowers that could bless you for having blest them and will love you for having loved them—flowers that have thoughts like yours and lives like yours; and which once saved, you save forever? Is this only a little power?"

The author might have had St Margaret in his mind as he wrote, for she, the perfect woman of flesh and blood, exemplifies all the beautiful things he says of womankind far better than any of the heroines of fiction, lovely as they are, of whom he speaks. St Margaret, Queen in every sense, understood her queenly power so well that the flowers indeed sprang up and blossomed in the paths she trod. She knew how to "go down among them"—among the poor and despairing and sinful—how to give them help and courage and revive sweet hopefulness in their sorrowful, crushed hearts, without losing aught of her own shining whiteness.

We have seen how she was loved for her goodness while she lived, and how for centuries after her death the women of Scotland looked on her as the model of all that was good and gracious. Not only in the homes of the poor was her name a household word, but in the stately dwellings of the noble and wealthy as well. Mothers of every rank told their daughters of sweet St Margaret's high ideals and fair example and sought to make them gentle and strong as she was, and the ladies of high degree who followed her as Queens of Scotland looked for no greater earthly glory than to be compared with the "good Queen."

It requires strength and fortitude to be a saint. There is unceasing warfare, if there is constant victory, and sometimes the signs of struggle show themselves in a suggestion of sternness, an unbending austerity that repels and frightens weaker mortals. Such goodness appears admirable indeed, but not always imitable—at least it does not invite imitation. St Margaret is strong and brave and fearless in her goodness, and yet her virtue never keeps us at a distance. She is a Queen, too, but her high station places no barrier between her and us. The more we study her life and character the more we feel her to be a friend. If she were in the "strong tower" of Dunfermline now, or high up in her fortress on the Castle rock in beautiful Edinburgh, it would seem but a natural thing for those in trouble and dire need to go to her. She is a woman like ourselves, with all her sanctity and high station, or, at least she is a woman such as any one of us might become if only we were as faithful to our graces as she was to hers.

"But we are not Queens," objects one little maiden. There you are making a mistake, my child. Every woman—and little maidens are the women of the future—is a queen. Each has a kingdom, large or small, subject to her rule, and it rests with herself whether she will seek through her queenly power, her own gratification and pleasure, or the happiness and welfare of her subjects. "The stars only may be over her head, the glow-worm in the night-cold grass may be the only fire at her feet; but home is yet wherever she is; and for a noble woman it stretches far round her, better than ceiled with cedar or painted with vermilion, shedding its quiet light far, for those who else were homeless."

High station and wealth are secondary considerations, little maiden. The queenly power is in yourself, be you rich or poor, princess or peasant, and it is well that you should recognise this early, and value the wonderful gift that God has given you. Do not waste your time dreaming of glorious things which you mean to do in the future. That was not St Margaret's way. "Act in the living present." Use now your little opportunities of being queenly, and then, when greater things have to be done, you will be ready for them.

God placed St Margaret high that her light might shine the farther, but if she had been a nun like her sister, or a noble lady in a lordly castle, or the toil-worn mistress of a lowly home, like one of those she gladdened in Dunfermline, she would still have been a queen. We should not have heard of her, perhaps, but Scotland would nevertheless have been better for her life. In any station she would have set self aside and sought the good of others, making her beneficent influence felt in ever widening circles outward to all the world, and this just because of her whole-hearted love of God and her desire to make others love Him.

Not every saint has had such constant love and homage as St Margaret. In her own age and in all the centuries that have passed since she lived, she has won devoted affection, and not alone from those who see spiritual things as she saw them, but from many others outside the Fold she loved so well. Perhaps the charm is her perfect womanliness. She is "incorruptibly good—instinctively, infallibly wise," but, always, with all this, she is a gentle, loving woman, full of kindly sympathy and tender helpfulness. Perfect in every aspect of her life, as daughter, sister, wife, mother and queen, history records no fault of hers and yet she understands human nature so well and has such marvellous patience with the weak and erring, that it is evident she has herself known struggle and warfare if she has never tasted the bitterness of defeat.

We have seen how she was loved and revered by husband, children and friends and how the fame of her good works travelled to other lands—not only to England but also beyond the sea to France and Italy and her own distant Hungary.

After her death mothers called their daughters by her name, hoping to see reproduced in them some of the virtues of their saintly namesake. Scottish girls of every degree in life were named "Margaret" in honour of the good Queen, and even in our own day, when the majority of Scots have been strangers to the faith of St Margaret for three hundred years the old custom is continued. Few Scottish families are without a "Mary" or a "Margaret" and many have both. True, the Scots do not name their girls in honour of St Mary or St Margaret either. The baby is "called after" mother, aunt, or grandmother, already so named, and who in like manner got their names from relatives. A few hundred years, however, would take any of them back to a gentle Catholic ancestor in the "days of faith" who called her child "Mary" or "Margaret" in honour of "Our Ladye Sainte Marie" or the "goode Queene," hoping that her little girl would grow up to imitate the virtues of the dear patron chosen for her.

Even now, (at time of first publication), in Protestant Scotland, St Margaret's name is loved and venerated. Needless to say, Catholics hold her dear as they have ever done, and so we pass over their devotion to her—the churches called by her name, the schools under her patronage, the constant prayers rising to her for the conversion of the land she loved. The remarkable thing is that Protestants who have, as far as they could, banished Our Lady herself from their native land, have only expressions of love and admiration for St Margaret. No name of higher inspiration could be found, when Glasgow University opened its doors to women, and the new College was named Queen Margaret's. Who can say but that the good Queen looks kindly on the institution? It may be that to her patronage is due much of the noble work done within its walls and by its students.

Protestant writers, and especially those connected with Fife, vie with each other in praising St Margaret. Looking, as they do, from the outside, they cannot understand and appreciate like Catholics, the spiritual beauty of her life, but they give her unstinted admiration and generously acknowledge her influence on Scottish womanhood in all succeeding generations.

"Perhaps there is no more beautiful character recorded in history," says Dr Skene in his *Celtic Scotland*, "than that of Margaret. For purity of motives, for a deep sense of religion, and great personal piety, for the unselfish performance of whatever duty lay before her, and for entire self-abnegation, she is unsurpassed."

Dr Boyd has his tribute also:—

There is but one story of her touching beauty, of her unselfish and holy life, of her wonderful influence over the rude people among whom it was appointed her to live.

But it is in Dunfermline that St Margaret's memory is most loved and honoured. Catholics, again, naturally, are foremost in devotion to her, and both church and school are St Margaret's, but Protestants also are proud of the sainted Queen whose memory sheds lustre through the mists of ages on their historic town.

Painters and poets seek inspiration from St Margaret's life, and love to call themselves her sons and daughters, and so the eleventh century Queen lives still in the country of her adoption teaching its children, as she taught their forefathers long ago, to love and reverence all that is beautiful and high and holy.

St Margaret came to Scotland eight hundred years ago and quickened the smouldering embers of our faith into a bright flame which glowed for five hundred years, and which is not extinguished yet, in spite of centuries of Protestantism. Nay! it is growing bright again.

"*They that instruct others unto justice, shall shine as stars for all eternity*" and St Margaret is thus shining now, close to the Sacred Heart of Jesus.

Sweet Saint of Scotland your power was great while you lived on earth. Surely in your radiant glory in high heaven, united as you are to Him you loved and served so faithfully here below, your influence is not diminished.

Our fathers needed your help in the eleventh century, but we, their sons and daughters of the twentieth century, need it more.

Pray for us, that we in our measure may help to spread the faith in our country, especially by the example of holy Catholic lives. Pray also for your truant children, wandering far from home and so blinded by the mists of error and prejudice that they cannot see their way. Bring them back, dear St Margaret, to your own loved faith, that, once again in Scotland, there may be "*one fold and one Shepherd.*" Pray for us all, that, like you, we may live only to love God and, that dying, we may join your sweet company, to live with Him and love Him for all eternity.

Saxon Princess! Margaret!
Given to us by the stormy sea,
The light of faith was dimming to darkness,
When God had pity and sent us thee.
Margaret of Scotland, hark to thy people,
Pleading from city and glen;
Look on us, pity us, pray for our country;
Win back our lost faith again.

Flower of the Southland! Margaret!
Storms have arisen and wrought us ill
Since thou wert planted in our wild Northland;
But lo! it glows with thy beauty still.

Queen of Scotland! Margaret!
Living for aye in our land art thou,
Reigning of old o'er our stern forefathers,
Throned in the hearts of their children now.

Pearl of women! Margaret!
The sunshine followed thy presence fair;
Sweet flowers sprang up where thy footsteps lingered,
For seeds of love had been scattered there.

Help of thy people! Margaret!
Scotland is calling for help again;
Blindly she seeks for her long-lost treasure—
Help, and her seeking will not be vain.

.

www.ingramcontent.com/pod-product-compliance
Lightning Source LLC
Chambersburg PA
CBHW031855090426
42741CB00005B/500